LOST

St. Helens Libraries

Please return / renew this item by the last date shown.
Books may also be renewed by phone and Internet.

Telephone – (01744) 676954 or 677822
Email – centrallibrary@sthelens.gov.uk
Online – http://eps.sthelens.gov.uk/rooms

385·094

COUNTRYSIDE BOOKS
NEWBURY, BERKSHIRE

COUNTRYSIDE BOOKS
3 Catherine Road
Newbury, Berkshire

ISBN 1 85306 828 4

To view our complete range of books,
please visit us at
www.countrysidebooks.co.uk

The cover picture shows the ex-LMS Pacific class locomotive 4-6-2,
no 46256, *Sir William Stanier*, FRS, hauling an express on the climb out
of Crewe from an original painting by Colin Doggett

Produced through MRM Associates Ltd., Reading
Printed by Woolnough Bookbinding Ltd., Irthlingborough

CONTENTS

ABBREVIATIONS

APT	Advanced Passenger Train
BL&CJR	Birkenhead, Lancashire & Cheshire Junction Railway
C&CR	Chester & Crewe Railway
C&HR	Chester & Holyhead Railway
C&WCJR	Chester & West Cheshire Junction Railway
CLC	Cheshire Lines Committee
CMR	Cheshire Midland Railway
DMU	Diesel Multiple Unit
DVT	Driving Van Trailer
EMU	Electric Multiple Unit
GCR	Great Central Railway
GJR	Grand Junction Railway
GNR	Great Northern Railway
GVT	Glyn Valley Tramway
GWR	Great Western Railway

H&BR&TCo	Hoylake & Birkenhead Rail & Tramway Company
L&BR	London & Birmingham Railway
LMS	London, Midland & Scottish Railway
LNER	London & North Eastern Railway
LNWR	London & North Western Railway
M&BR	Manchester & Birmingham Railway
M&DJR	Mold & Denbigh Junction Railway
MB&M	Macclesfield, Bollington & Marple Railway
MR	Midland Railway
MS&LR	Manchester, Sheffield & Lincolnshire Railway
NRM	National Railway Museum
NSR	North Staffordshire Railway
NWMR	North Wales Mineral Railway
OE&WR	Oswestry, Ellesmere & Whitchurch Railway
S&BR	Shrewsbury & Birmingham Railway
S&CLER	Southport & Cheshire Lines Extension Railway
S&CR	Shrewsbury & Chester Railway
S&WJR	Stockport & Woodley Junction Railway
SH&DR	Seacombe, Hoylake & Deeside Railway
SO&CJR	Shrewsbury, Oswestry & Chester Junction Railway
SR	Southern Railway
ST&AJR	Stockport, Timperley & Altrincham Junction Railway
W&NR	Warrington & Newton Railway
WCML	West Coast Main Line
WCR	West Cheshire Railway
WM&CQR	Wrexham, Mold & Connah's Quay Railway

ACKNOWLEDGEMENTS

Acknowledgements and thanks go to libraries at Chester, Frodsham, Macclesfield, Runcorn, Manchester and Oswestry for their support. Thanks for the many early photographs go to the late John Smith of 'Lens of Sutton', D.K. Jones, the Staffordshire County Museum at Shugborough and the City Central Library at Hanley.

Thanks also go the following who generously contributed information:
Cheshire County Council, Engineering Consultancy; Cheshire County Council, Countryside Management; Stockport Heritage Services, Director of Leisure Services; Wrexham County Borough, Chief Transportation & Engineering Officer; British Rail, Public Affairs Department, London; Railtrack PLC, Rail House, Manchester; Merseyrail Electrics, Customer Relations, Liverpool; North West Regional Railway, Store Street, Manchester; The Railway Age, Crewe; Churnet Valley Railway, Cheddleton, Leek; the Brighton Belle public house, Middlewich Road, Winsford; William Jack of Market Drayton; Wm. R. Hawkin and Neville S. Kiernan of Frodsham; Robin Butterell, Organiser, Eaton Hall Railway Centenary Exhibition.

Finally personal thanks go to the late Vernon Deadman who helped with locomotive identification and to Joan, my wife, for travelling Cheshire with me and for her careful checking of the final manuscript.

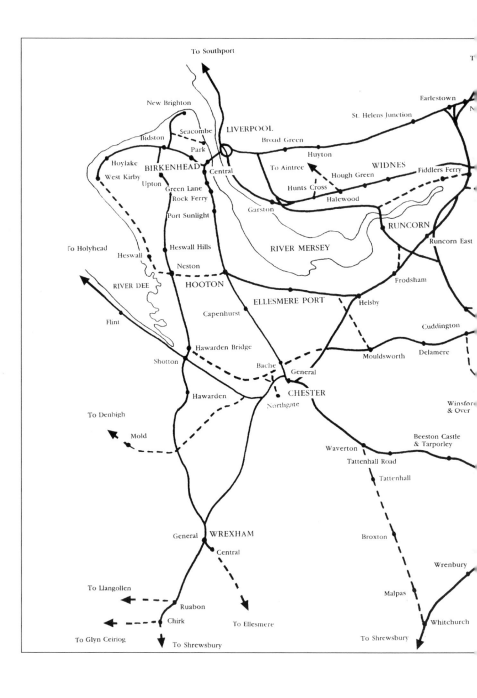

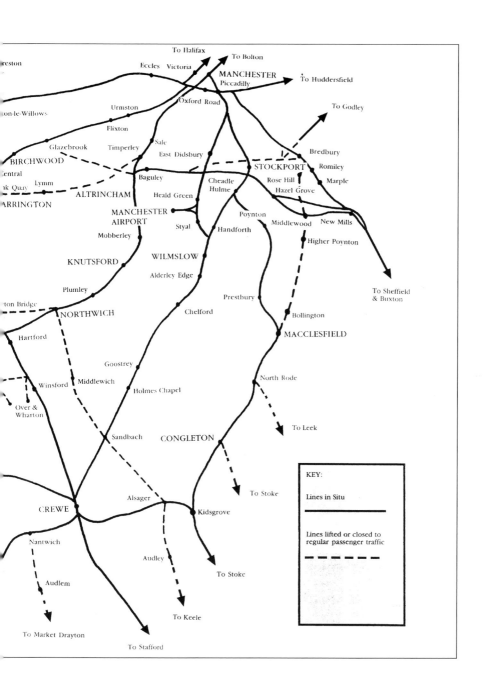

To Halifax
To Bolton
reston
Eccles Victoria
MANCHESTER
Piccadilly
To Huddersfield
Oxford Road
Urmston
To Godley
on-le-Willows
Flixton
Sale
Glazebrook Timperley
East Didsbury
Bredbury
BIRCHWOOD
STOCKPORT
Romiley
entral
Baguley
Cheadle
Rose Hill
Marple
Lymm
Hulme
ak Quay
ALTRINCHAM
Heald Green
Hazel Grove
ARRINGTON
MANCHESTER
Poynton
New Mills
AIRPORT
Styal
Middlewood
Handforth
Mobberley
Higher Poynton
KNUTSFORD
WILMSLOW
Alderley Edge
To Sheffield
Plumley
Prestbury
& Buxton
ton Bridge
Chelford
Bollington
NORTHWICH
Hartford
MACCLESFIELD
Goostrey
Winsford Middlewich
North Rode
Holmes Chapel
Over &
Wharton
To Leek
Sandbach
CONGLETON
Alsager
To Stoke
CREWE
Kidsgrove
Nantwich
Audley
Audlem
To Stoke
To Keele
To Market Drayton
To Stafford

KEY:

Lines in Situ

_____

Lines lifted or closed to
regular passenger traffic

- - - - -

BIBLIOGRAPHY

In compiling *Cheshire Railways Remembered*, I have referred to numerous sources, many now out of print, which include the following and which can be recommended for further reading:

Baughan, Peter E. *A Regional History of the Railways of Great Britain, Vol ll, North and Mid Wales* (David & Charles)

Bolger, Paul *Railway Stations, Merseyside and District* (Bluecoat Press)

Cheshire Federation of Women's Institutes *The Cheshire Village Book* (Countryside Books & CFWI, Chester)

Christiansen, Rex *A Regional History of the Railways of Great Britain, Vol 7, The West Midlands* (David & Charles)

Christiansen, Rex *Forgotten Railways: The West Midlands* (David & Charles)

Christiansen, Rex *Rail Centres: Crewe* (Ian Allan)

Dyckhoff, Nigel *The Cheshire Lines Committee, Then and Now* (Ian Allan)

Griffiths, R.P. *The Cheshire Lines Railway* (The Oakwood Press)

Holt, Geoffrey O. *A Regional History of the Railways of Great Britain, Vol 10, The North West* (David & Charles)

Reed, Brian *Crewe to Carlisle* (Ian Allan)

Shannon, Paul & Hillmer, John *British Railways: Past & Present, No 6, Cheshire & North Wales* (Past & Present Publishing Ltd)

Williams, Herbert *Railways in Wales* (Christopher Davies, Swansea)

Introduction

When the railways came in the early 19th century it seemed that the drudgery of travel along poor roads and the slowness of canal traffic would be at an end. But this great new idea had its opponents. An article written in 1836 read: 'I foresee what the effect will be – it will set the world a-gadding. Twenty miles an hour! Why, you will not be able to keep an apprentice boy at work; every Saturday evening he must take a trip to spend the Sabbath with his sweetheart. Grave plodding citizens will be flying about like comets. All local attractions will be at an end.'

History tells us of course this was far from the truth. Conventional railways as known today began in 1825 with the establishment of the Stockton & Darlington Railway. The well-known Rainhill trials were held in 1829 on the Liverpool & Manchester Railway and won by George Stephenson's famous locomotive *Rocket*. By 1833 a spate of railway bills was before Parliament, the most important of these being for the London & Birmingham Railway, primarily intended to provide the rapid transport of cheap food for London's fast growing population.

Queen Victoria came to the throne in 1837 just as railways were beginning to link the great centres of population and industry across Britain. That same year the Grand Junction Railway (GJR) opened with lines across Cheshire and linking the Liverpool & Manchester Railway with Birmingham. When the London & Birmingham Railway (L&BR) opened throughout on 17th September 1838, Britain's first trunk railway out of the capital was born.

The GJR proved profitable and other lines soon followed, many of them taking advantage of Cheshire's salt-production industry. Further major routes opened linking the Merseyside docks and Manchester with Chester and Crewe. When the Chester & Holyhead Railway opened, London was linked with Dublin.

From these main routes, branch lines developed. Steam trains made their way across open stretches of countryside, linking remote villages and towns. In many instances passenger traffic remained light throughout, although goods or mineral traffic provided essential services. Some lines suffered an early demise simply because they became uneconomic and, with road transport fast competing, the Beeching cuts of the early 1960s took a heavy toll.

This book intends to examine the lives of the many lines in Cheshire as well as the decline and closure of many 'lost' today. *Lost Railways of Cheshire* provides the reader with a means to find numerous closed stations and the many trackbeds that have survived, some converted to footpaths.

Leslie Oppitz

1
Crewe – The Beginnings

Crewe station owes its existence to the Grand Junction Railway (GJR) which opened between Birmingham and Warrington on 4th July 1837. A reporter from *The Times* travelling on the first train on the morning of the opening day reported, 'The train arrived at Crewe at three minutes to nine o'clock and was received with a hearty welcome by a large concourse of spectators collected together for the occasion.' The *Crewe Guardian* covered the event by reporting, 'There was great

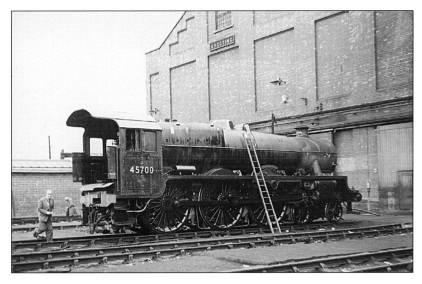

Ex-LMS 5XP Jubilee class locomotive minus tender receives attention at Crewe Works in August 1962. Built in 1936, it was originally named 'Britannia' but was renamed 'Amethyst' after the frigate involved in the 1949 Yangtze river incident. (D.K. Jones)

Platform 1 Crewe station c1910. The roof of the building just visible above the first coach is signal box A which survives today at The Railway Age site. (Lens of Sutton)

rejoicing in the neighbourhood and people came from all over the countryside to witness the strange spectacle. At various points on the line the country folk ran out of their houses to see the strange iron monster go past and wondered what next would be witnessed?'

The station began in a small way. For its first three years after opening in 1837, six trains a day in each direction stopped there for omnibus or carriage connections to Sandbach or Nantwich. There was only one cross-over between up and down tracks, this being opposite the station's one engine shed. This had accommodation for just one engine, always held in steam in case of need.

Crewe began as an operating centre in 1840 when the Chester and Crewe Railway (C&CR) arrived. Two years later, on 10th August 1842, Manchester & Birmingham Railway (M&BR) trains reached Crewe. On 1st January 1846 the M&BR, the L&BR and the GJR amalgamated to become the London & North Western Railway (LNWR). The LNWR always claimed that it created

Platform 1 (renumbered platform 14) photographed in August 1996. Signal box A has gone and the track is used merely to connect with adjacent sidings. (Author)

Crewe as a railway town but the GJR had done much for the town. The GJR built over 200 railway houses and established a locomotive carriage and wagon works, having moved it to Crewe from Edge Hill, Liverpool. Locomotive building began in 1845.

Nevertheless the LNWR continued to make Crewe the famous railway town it became. By 1861 the town's population had doubled to nearly 18,000 and by the end of the century it had passed 40,000, many working for the LNWR. The railway company provided many services in the town including gas and water supplies, a hospital and a church. Christ Church was built in 1843 and consecrated in 1845. It was partly demolished in 1977 but it re-opened two years later. Today its striking tower remains a reminder of the early GJR days. Crewe works even had a brickworks of its own providing materials not only for houses in the town but also for use elsewhere in the LNWR system.

To the south of Crewe station extensive goods facilities were

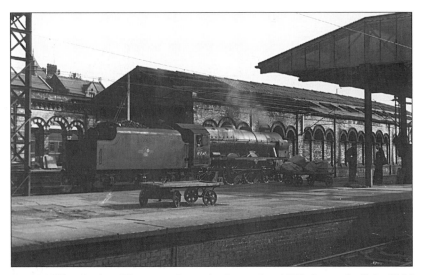

Ex-LMS locomotive 'Planet' at Crewe in September 1959. It was built in 1934 as one of the Patriot 5XP class engines and was named 'Planet' when rebuilt with a larger boiler. (D.K. Jones)

established together with large carriage sidings. In addition large engine sheds were built to the north and south of the town to provide locomotives to meet the increasing goods and freight requirements. The North shed, located where the Chester line left the West Coast Main Line (WCML), housed express engines and in addition heavy maintenance and repair work was carried out. The South shed, built in the 1890s, was close to the marshalling yard and met demands for goods locomotives needed locally, as well as receiving 'visitors' including Great Western Railway (GWR) locomotives working from the West Midlands and Shrewsbury areas.

As the railways declined with the introduction of road traffic, so Crewe changed. Immediately prior to the Second World War Rolls-Royce built an aircraft engine factory which produced Merlin engines used to power Spitfire fighters. After the war the factory switched to the manufacture of quality cars although this work, like the railways, eventually went into decline.

Further changes came in 1961 with the completion of the first section of electrification between Manchester and Crewe,

The Crewe Arms Hotel close to the station was built in 1837 by Lord Crewe. Queen Victoria and her suite stayed there in 1848 when travelling by rail south from Scotland. (Author)

followed by the Liverpool section in 1962. Crewe North shed closed in May 1965 with the site later to become a large car park. Crewe South shed survived until November 1967 and on 4th April 1968 the area had its last steam visitor, no 70013 *Oliver Cromwell*.

In 1985 Crewe station was extensively remodelled, giving a much faster through running of trains. This was a multi-million pound programme which included improved services for passengers as well as the upgrading of signalling and track layouts. Two years later, on 24th July 1987, Crewe celebrated 150 years as a railway centre. A festival to mark the event included the opening by the Queen of the Crewe Heritage Centre (now known as The Railway Age).

Not far from Crewe station can be found the Crewe Arms originally built in 1837 by Lord Crewe. It was described as 'very fair accommodation and often providing, about one o'clock, a fine hot joint of grass-fed beef of magnificent dimensions'. In

September 1848 Queen Victoria and her suite stayed there having given the inn-keeper no notice of arrival. The Queen was travelling south from Scotland by train and decided to break her 'tedious journey' at Crewe. In 1864 the hotel was leased to the LNWR which had the building enlarged although retaining its original style architecture. The Crewe Arms Hotel survives today, once again in private hands.

Recalling Crewe's phenomenal growth as a railway town, the *Crewe Guardian* wrote in 1887, 'Fifty years ago the place where Crewe is now located was nothing more than a small hamlet, a few labourers' cottages scattered about, and farms dotted here and there like currants in a penny bun...'

Crewe Sorting Office

In the late 1960s Crewe handled some three million letters and around 200,000 parcels each week with most of it arriving or leaving by rail. Mail trains at Crewe were big business with postal trains arriving late at night. Often staff had less than 15 minutes to load and unload local mail, transfer sacks from one train to another and if necessary split one train up and join two others together.

The GJR introduced a mail service to Crewe in 1838 with a travelling post office adapted from a horse box. The first mail-sorting carriage soon followed plus apparatus to pick up and drop mail at speed. Amounts of mail grew over the years and trains such as 'The Irish Mail' or the 'West Coast Postal Express' could be seen. As trains pulled in, so streams of postal workers appeared from nowhere to hump mailbags in various directions.

W.H. Auden's (1907–1973) poem on the Night Mail describes the service:

This is the Night Mail crossing the Border,
Bringing the cheque and the postal order...

Pulling up Beattock, a steady climb:
The gradient's against her, but she's on time...

Birds turn their heads as she approaches,
Stare from the bushes at her blank-faced coaches.

But changes are already taking place. A £150 million container centre opened on 30th September 1996 at Willesden, north of London, to become a road-rail interchange and postal station covering almost the whole of South-East England. Smaller units will cover the rest of the country including a rail hub planned at Warrington with rail access from a siding just to the north of Warrington Bank Quay station. Sadly for many, when this happens Crewe will no longer be the major sorting centre that it was. Almost 160 years of history will have slipped by.

The Advanced Passenger Train (APT) introduced on the West Coast Main Line in 1979 did not prove successful and was withdrawn in 1983. It is preserved today at The Railway Age site. (Author)

19

Crewe station signal box A is today preserved at its Railway Age site. Built by the LNWR in 1907, it was modernised by LMS and BR and taken out of service in 1985. The larger GWR box behind came from Exeter West. (Author)

The Railway Age, Crewe

The Railway Age is about a 20 minute walk from Crewe station and a visit is recommended. Here it is possible to see numerous ex-BR diesel locomotives as well as industrial side-tank and tank engines and many items of rolling stock. Pride of place is given in the exhibition hall to the former LNWR steam locomotive 2-2-2 *Cornwall* no 3020 (on loan from NRM) which was built at Crewe works in 1847.

The centre also includes the Advanced Passenger Train (APT) which was introduced in 1979 to provide quicker journey times on the West Coast Main Line (WCML). It was reckoned the APT could reach 155 mph and also improve speeds by up to 40% on curves using the tilt. But it did not prove successful and it was relegated to passenger relief services from 1983 to 1985. After

1985 the APT was used for development purposes for future electric locomotives, assisting particularly in the construction of Class 91 locomotives and Mk IV coaches which were put in service on the East Coast Main Line.

But it seems all is not lost for high-speed tilting trains. Proposals are being considered to use such diesel services on the Trans-Pennine route linking Liverpool and Manchester with Leeds, Middlesborough and Newcastle. With passenger numbers soaring since the opening of Manchester Airport, it is considered tilting trains could boost traffic even further.

Crewe station signal box A survives on The Railway Age site. Built by the LNWR in 1907 it originally stood opposite platform 1 (now platform 14) at Crewe station controlling semaphore signals and points using miniature levers. Modernised by the LMS and BR it was taken out of service in 1985 and moved to its present location.

The centre is a good reminder of the times when Crewe was a great railway town. It also helps to recall the great days of steam by acting as a stabling point for numerous preserved locomotives which operate special trains from Crewe to Holyhead or on the Settle and Carlisle line.

2
The Grand Junction Railway

Birmingham/Stafford/Crewe/Warrington

Passengers travelling the West Coast Main Line (WCML) today may take for granted a five hour journey in comparative comfort from London Euston to Glasgow Central. Yet in much earlier times conditions were far from InterCity standards. Soon after the opening of the Grand Junction Railway (GJR), trains consisted of first and second class coaches as well as open third class coaches. Only first and second class gave protection from the weather and the latter had no lining or cushions on the seat. Some coaches even had seats on the roof for those who preferred

Ex-LMS class 5XP locomotive 'Private Sykes V.C.' at Crewe in 1958. It acquired the name Private Sykes from a LNWR employee who was decorated during the 1914-1918 war. (D.K. Jones)

Acton Bridge station c1910 when trains stopped frequently between Crewe and Liverpool or Warrington. A branch (now closed) from Acton Bridge also carried trains via Northwich and Middlewich to Crewe. (Lens of Sutton)

riding outside. Fortunately there were few tunnels – one of 100 yards near Preston Brook must have given an uncomfortable journey!

As early as 1838 the GJR introduced a 'convertible bed carriage', which eventually led to the modern sleeping car. The comfort of steam heating came first in 1843 although initially applied only to Queen Victoria's Royal Saloon. Fifty years later in 1893 the LNWR's Wolverton works began constructing corridor-vestibuled coaches for the Euston to Glasgow service, gaining them the nickname of 'The Corridor'.

Only one station survives today between Stafford and Crewe. This is Norton Bridge, a short island platform where trains leave on the former North Staffordshire Railway (NSR) branch to Stone and Stoke. Back on the WCML, Madeley and Whitmore stations closed to passengers in 1952 but they were once of some importance with horse-drawn coaches offering services to and from the Potteries. Next came Betley Road station serving the nearby village of Betley. In the 1920s Betley Road saw only three

Acton Bridge, August 1996. The buildings and station yard have long since gone. Although today dozens of trains pass through daily, only 13 in each direction stop at the station. (Author)

trains each way daily (Stafford to Crewe). It closed in 1945.

Basford station closed much earlier, in 1875, to make way for track improvements, the area later to become the extensive Basford Hall Marshalling Yard. This was an LNWR project which initially employed over 600 men and could handle a daily intake of some 600 wagons. At its peak in the 1930s it was reckoned the yard handled more than 400 trains daily and nearly 50,000 wagons a week. In the 1960s Basford Yard was reconstructed and electrified.

Crewe station is probably one of the most famous worldwide. Before the GJR arrived the town had a population of just 184 but when locomotive building began in 1845 the town's future was assured. The LNWR, known as 'The Premier Line', was soon to employ more than 10,000 at Crewe. The station has of course seen many changes. From its modest beginnings, track improvements have been implemented over the years and within the

Until April 1998 this coach of the once famous 'Brighton Belle' served as a restaurant extension at the Brighton Belle public house at Winsford. Named 'Mona' it has subsequently undergone renovation by its new owner, the Venice-Simplon Orient Express. In its time passengers have included the late Queen Mother, travelling between London and Brighton. (Author)

1990s a West Coast modernisation programme was put in hand to upgrade track and signalling to raise maximum speeds to a potential of 125 mph. Earlier modernisation in 1985 at Crewe meant that six signalboxes were closed.

Only three stations have survived between Crewe and Warrington Bank Quay, these being Winsford, Hartford and Acton Bridge. Not far from Winsford station in Middlewich Road can be found a coach of the former *Brighton Belle*, forming part of the popular Brighton Belle public house. Here one can enjoy first-class meals at the tables which originally existed in the first-class compartments. The coach, one of a number, began its life in 1932 on the newly electrified line between London and Brighton, running three times each way daily doing the 51 mile journey in exactly 60 minutes. The coaches were withdrawn from service in 1972 after 40 years sterling service. The Winsford

Inside the coach at the Brighton Belle. The pub displays many items of railway memorabilia and a visit is recommended. (Author)

coach, named 'Mona', had among its distinguished guests the late Queen Mother travelling between London and Brighton in 1948. 'Mona' was removed from Winsford in April 1998 to join its sister coach 'Audrey', both now the property of the Venice-Simplon Orient Express.

Hartford owes its existence to the fact that last century its inhabitants included the chairman of the Grand Junction Railway and it was because of him that mainline trains were stopped! Coppenhall station just north of Crewe lasted only three years, closing in 1840, whereas Minshull Vernon lasted until 1942, closing during World War II. Moore, close to the Bridgewater Canal, closed a year later in 1943. It was not far from Moore station that steam enthusiasts may recall water troughs between the lines to enable tender scoops to pick up water without stopping. Passengers close to the engine may well have been advised to close the compartment windows to avoid the spray that resulted! Preston Brook lived out its London, Midland & Scottish Railway (LMS) days, lasting until 1948.

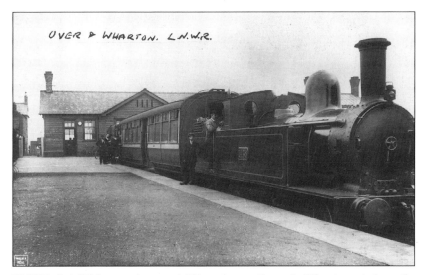

LNWR 2-4-2T locomotive no 1458 waits at Over & Wharton station, the terminus to a one mile branch from Winsford. The line opened in 1882 and was mostly used for salt traffic. (Lens of Sutton)

The one mile long branch to Wharton from Winsford junction on the main line, opened in 1882 to take advantage of the salt traffic for which the town was well known. The station was called Over & Wharton to avoid confusion with a Cheshire Lines Committee (CLC) station in the town of the same name. The line was never a busy one with the shuttle between Over & Wharton and Hartford taking just seven minutes with five trains each way daily and none on Sundays.

At Weaver junction tracks to Liverpool leave the WCML. Further north the WCML crosses and then joins the line from Chester to Manchester before reaching Warrington Bank Quay station. Warrington's first railway station opened as early as 1831. It was built by the Warrington & Newton Railway (W&NR), incorporated in 1829, which ran trains from Newton (later known as Earlestown) to Dallam Lane in Warrington.

The 4¼ mile branch opened in 1831 mostly to cater for passenger traffic to Haydock Park races. Dallam Lane station building was two-storied and built of red brick. It has been written that an adjacent public house, the Three Pigeons, served

Warrington Bank Quay in earlier times. The station served LNWR trains and prior to 1963 stairs connected with a low-level station on a little used line between Liverpool and Manchester. (Lens of Sutton)

for a time as goods office and for the sale of W&NR tickets but subsequent research considers this unlikely. The Three Pigeons lay at an outer end of the station area and it is considered that most passengers would have approached the station from the opposite Foundry Lane end. Just north of Dallam Street a further short W&NR branch opened to the Mersey at Bank Quay in 1835, initially used for just coal and freight traffic. The GJR took over the W&NR in 1835 and when its lines reached Warrington in 1837 the role reversed with Bank Quay handling the passenger traffic.

In 1868 the GJR (LNWR from 1846) Bank Quay station closed, replaced by a two-level Bank Quay station about ¼ mile to the south. This gave a passenger connection by stairs to a low-level LNWR station on the Liverpool to Manchester line which closed in 1963. This line has remained open for freight traffic.

Today Warrington Bank Quay is well served with InterCity trains between London and the North and also to the West Country. The station also handles trains operating between

28

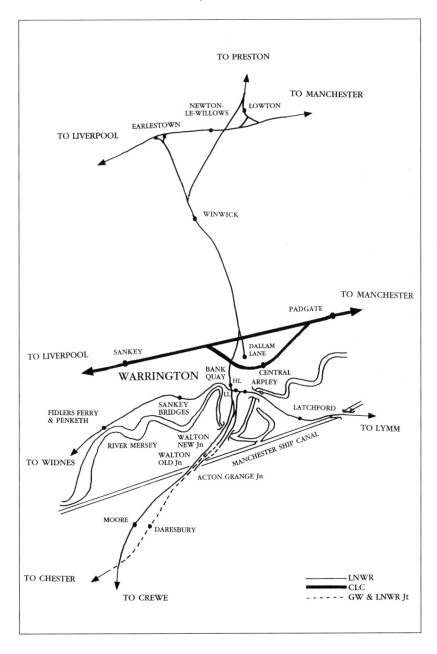

Chester and Manchester Victoria/Oxford Road using what was once the GWR/LNWR joint line from Chester to Warrington. Northwards from Bank Quay, trains cross the former Cheshire Lines Committee tracks before reaching Winwick junction where lines separate to either carry trains northwards to Preston or towards Earlestown and then eastwards to Manchester (Victoria).

Warrington Bank Quay, August 1996, serving frequent InterCity trains between London and the North as well as a Chester/Manchester service. The former factory buildings have been replaced by Lever Brothers where buildings dwarf the station. (Author)

3
Further Lines From Crewe

Crewe/Chester; Crewe/Kidsgrove/Stoke,
Crewe/Runcorn/Liverpool

The former Waverton station between Crewe and Chester. Rebuilt in 1898 by the Duke of Westminster, it lasted until closure in 1959 to become in 1996 the offices of Morrey Transport. (Author)

Crewe/Chester

There was tragedy at Waverton, just four miles south-east of Chester, on 2nd July 1971, when a special train carrying school

Beeston Castle & Tarporley station, close to the Shropshire Union Canal. The station closed in 1966 and today no stations have survived between Crewe and Chester. (Lens of Sutton)

parties returning from Wales was derailed. Hot weather had caused the track to buckle and, as a result of the accident, two children died.

Before the railways came goods were carried by barges, or 'flats' as they were called, along the 18th-century Ellesmere and Chester Canal which cuts straight through Waverton village. The barges carried corn from the farms along the canal to a mill where it was ground. The mill survives but it has become a marina and caravan centre.

The Chester & Crewe Railway (C&CR) received Parliamentary approval on 30th June 1837 but three months before its completion it was taken over by the Grand Junction Railway (GJR). It was not difficult to build over its 21 miles, with much of the route running close to the Shropshire Union Canal. When services began on 1st October 1840 the movement of goods became easier, improving the carriage of farm produce to the nearby towns.

There were intermediate stations at Worleston (Nantwich until

All that remains of Beeston Castle & Tarporley is the cobbled station approach and the area which supported the awning's pillars. The station house still stands adjacent. (Author)

1858), Calveley, Beeston Castle & Tarporley, Tattenhall Road and Waverton. Waverton's first railway station, known as 'Black Dog', closed in 1898 to be replaced by another, 41 chains to the west. On 15th June 1959 this too closed to passenger traffic, a victim of Dr Beeching. But the station building, rebuilt in distinctive style in 1897 by the Duke of Westminster, is still there as the offices of Morrey Transport. Originally there were buildings either side of the track but the opposite side was demolished. The surviving building had a canopy which stretched over the track but this has now gone. Waverton station's main feature is its fascinating spiral chimneys.

Tattenhall Road station was first known as 'Crow's Nest' but was finally named just Tattenhall when the Chester/Whitchurch branch closed in 1957 (see chapter 14). Today all the stations along the line have gone. The last to go were Beeston Castle & Tarporley and Tattenhall, both of which closed in 1966.

Alsager station c1910 on what was formerly a North Staffordshire Railway (NSR) line between Kidsgrove and Crewe. This is the only station on the route to survive. (Lens of Sutton)

Crewe/Kidsgrove/Stoke

The short 8½ mile line from Crewe to Kidsgrove was originally a product of the North Staffordshire Railway (NSR) which aimed for a link between the LNWR's West Coast Main Line and Eastern England. Authorised in June 1846, the NSR soon ran into difficulties when Lord Crewe raised objections over a proposed route. As a result the NSR was compelled to submit a revised route to Parliament which required the tracks to leave the Crewe main line three miles to the south and then rejoin the originally planned route at Radway Green. This was approved by Parliament in July 1847.

Passenger and freight services began on 9th October 1848 but initially, because of disputes with the LNWR, traffic was light. Today the line carries passenger services between Crewe and Skegness via Stoke and Nottingham. The track between Crewe and Radway Green has been singled, Radway Green having closed in 1966. Electrification has been considered but, with inadequate support, the idea has foundered.

Alsager station, today the only intermediate station between Crewe and Kidsgrove, has survived. In 1996 the station's southern buildings and canopy which in part date back to 1848 were saved from demolition. This is thanks to funds made available which include a contribution from Congleton Borough Council. The buildings on the northern side have been let for community use.

Prior to 1944 Kidsgrove station (in Staffordshire) was known as Harecastle but today Harecastle station is no more. When the route from Euston to the North West was electrified in the 1960s, the three tunnels south of Harecastle were found to be too narrow for present day stock. One tunnel (Harecastle North) was demolished and the remaining two were abandoned. British Rail constructed a loop and built Kidsgrove station at a new site.

A local resident who lived in the Chatterley area (north of Stoke) recalls his first family holiday back in the earlier days of steam. The journey first entailed a train to Crewe where he says they 'changed from the severe austerity of the North Staffordshire Railway to the magnificent luxury of the London & North Western'. Another journey recalled, overnight on this occasion, was from Crewe to Aberystwyth in a gas-lit clerestory Great Western Railway coach and his 'being sick on Machynlleth station in the cold grey hours of dawn'!

Crewe/Runcorn/Liverpool

Before the railways came it was possible to carry a ton of goods between Liverpool and Manchester for 6/- on the Runcorn Canal. This compared with £2 per ton by packhorse. The 3rd Duke of Bridgewater foresaw a great future in canal traffic and with this in mind he built waterways linking coal pits with Manchester and the Mersey estuary at Runcorn. This had the effect of halving the price of coal in Manchester to 4d a hundredweight. The railway builders derived great benefit from the earlier canal navigators, drawing on their experience to build tunnels, viaducts and so forth.

The midday mail train approaches Runcorn station. The nearby Runcorn bridge was built between 1864 and 1869 giving direct access to Liverpool. Services across the bridge began in April 1869. (Lens of Sutton)

When the LNWR opened a line from Edge Hill to Garston, joining the St Helens line at Speke junction, the advantages of bridging the river Mersey became greater. Such a line would shorten the route from Liverpool Lime Street to Crewe by over eight miles and also avoid the congested tracks through Warrington. Work on Runcorn bridge began in April 1864, taking five years before completion. The three girder spans each measured 305 ft and they were constructed, piece by piece, on the site. The approach viaduct from the Liverpool side rose steeply to a height of 75 ft and required 59 arches. Plaques over the portals commemorate William Baker, the engineer responsible.

Passenger services across the great bridge began on 1st April 1869. Those responsible little realised that a century later this was to provide a major link between Crewe and Liverpool for the hundreds of InterCity trains that travel to London Euston as well as other parts of the country.

The trains from Liverpool joined the WCML at Dutton where the LNWR's first 'flying junction' was constructed, built to avoid

36

tracks actually crossing each other thus causing unnecessary delays. Probably to avoid confusion with Ditton across the river, the LNWR named the signal box Weaver Junction and not Dutton Junction. In his book, *A Regional History of the Railways of Great Britain Volume 10 The North West*, Geoffrey O. Holt amusingly points out that it can be said the new line 'ran from Ditton to Dutton'.

Even though the route from Liverpool to Crewe was now shorter, passengers were not allowed a reduction in fares. This was a situation agreed by Parliament to ensure that the railway company did not lose any revenue after constructing Runcorn bridge. In the same way, pedestrians saw little financial benefit. A footbridge had been built alongside the tracks but users had to pay a toll.

South of Frodsham a connection of less than two miles was built to link with the Chester to Warrington line. This allowed frequent services between Liverpool Lime Street and Chester. Today the line is no longer used for passenger traffic.

After crossing the Chester to Warrington line (underneath in Sutton tunnel), Liverpool to Crewe trains passed close to the villages of Sutton and Aston. A station called Sutton Weaver opened there but this only lasted until November 1931. The area is currently swallowed up by Runcorn developments.

4
Lines Reach Manchester

Chester/Warrington/Manchester;
Crewe/Wilmslow/Manchester

Chester/Warrington/Manchester

Without the sophisticated signalling systems of today, early trains relied on what was called a 'time interval system'. In those days this seemed satisfactory in principle but trains were sometimes liable to break down or stall on gradients. This placed a great responsibility on the guard who was obliged to protect his train by running back down the line laying detonators. More often than not the driver got his engine moving again and the guard was left behind. Because of this the guard would often make his way to the engine to confer, thus leaving the rear totally unprotected. A further complication was the inaccuracy of many station clocks. Some kept 'local time' despite recommendations from the Board of Trade that 'London time' should be observed (later known as 'railway time').

Part of the line between Chester General and Warrington was constructed by the Birkenhead, Lancashire & Cheshire Junction Railway (BL&CJR). The company was floated in 1846 with the idea of building a line from Hooton via Helsby and Frodsham to cross the Grand Junction Railway south of Warrington, thus reaching Manchester's industrial areas. This did not happen, instead the BL&CJR joined the GJR south of Warrington (see chapter 9).

There were many delays in construction mostly due to shortage of funds. Completion dates were set and passed. During the line's progress a change of route was made at

A class 158 DMU leaves Sutton tunnel between Frodsham and Runcorn East. In April 1851 the tunnel was the scene of a terrible disaster which cost nine lives and many injuries. (Author)

Frodsham which placed the station actually in the town, causing further delays and extra costs. The line was eventually opened on 31st October 1850, although public services did not begin until 18th December 1850. Three trains daily ran in each direction between Chester and Manchester Victoria, providing a more direct route for passengers travelling from Manchester to North Wales or Ireland.

It was not long after opening that the line proved very popular with racegoers. 30th April 1851 was Chester Cup Day when some 4,000 people crowded onto trains at Manchester Victoria anxious to reach Chester's Roodee racecourse. Because of the unexpected large numbers trains ran late, one arriving at Chester 2½ hours behind time!

It was such a train that was involved in a serious accident in the 1 mile 176 yds Sutton tunnel (between Frodsham and Runcorn East) on 30th April 1851 when carrying racegoers back to Manchester after the races. In a booklet produced by the

Runcorn East station opened on 3rd October 1983, funded by British Rail, Cheshire County Council and Warrington & Runcorn Development Corporation. It is linked to the unique Runcorn Busway which provides frequent services to most parts of the town. (Author)

Frodsham & District Local History Group, Wm. R. Hawkin writes that the train involved left Chester on a wet day with about 430 passengers on board. A second train carrying some 900 passengers crammed into 18 small carriages left shortly afterwards.

At Frodsham the first train stopped for passengers to alight but the rain had turned to sleet with the result that when the train reached an incline the engine's 5 ft 6 in diameter wheels began to slip. Despite the rails being sanded, the train came to a halt near Sutton tunnel by which time the second train had caught it up. When they were within visual range, the first train's guard requested a 'push' from the second. They proceeded slowly until about the middle of the tunnel where the gradient again became adverse, then both engines' wheels slipped and the two trains came to a halt.

This was now a highly dangerous situation because a further

40

Chester General station when the city had two railway stations. Chester Northgate closed in 1969. (Lens of Sutton)

train given clearance on the 'time interval system' was due to leave Frodsham. The driver – an experienced man – related how he entered Sutton tunnel at 15 to 20 miles per hour not noticing anything out of the ordinary. He said, 'I saw a lot of steam which, half way through, got very thick. I didn't think this extraordinary but I shut some steam off and went rather slower. The next thing I perceived was that I had run into a number of coaches before me.' He had in fact struck a flat truck with a private carriage on it. Inside were the owner's coachman and footman. Miraculously both survived.

Others were less fortunate. Five people were killed outright and four died later, whilst between 30 and 40 were injured, some seriously. It was reported that 'fearful confusion ensued; 1,600 passengers found themselves crowded together in perfect darkness'. This was worsened by the sound of yet another train approaching but fortunately a guard managed to get back along the line with a red tail light and stop it in time. An inquest recorded a verdict of accidental death of the victims but added the feelings that 'the management of the railway in question was imperfect and inefficient, thereby endangering the safety of the public'.

41

Recommendations were made and followed. Yet the accident was recalled for many years by local folk. There is a tale that when, many years later, repairs were carried out to the tunnel, gold coins were found which could have been the winnings from the punters at the races.

In 1859 the BL&CJR became known as the Birkenhead Railway. In November 1860 it was absorbed jointly by the GWR and the LNWR to become known as the GW & LNWR Joint line. In 1942 a wartime connection was made with nearby Cheshire Lines Committee tracks (see chapter 6) but when Chester Northgate closed in 1969 the junction was reversed so trains could use Chester General.

Crewe/Wilmslow/Manchester

The Manchester & Birmingham Railway (M&BR) could more aptly be called the 'Manchester & Crewe'. The company's original intention was to reach London without running on GJR lines, even to the point of laying tracks parallel for part of the journey. But the M&BR decided it could not finance such a costly scheme so the GJR proposed the M&BR should build a line to Crewe and then run its own trains southwards.

Once the amended M&BR route was agreed by Parliament, the GJR withdrew the M&BR's right to use its tracks and bitter arguments followed. When the M&BR line opened in May 1842, tempers were still running high and trains ran only to Sandbach. Negotiations over the next three months were needed to resolve the problem and even then the M&BR was only granted a bay at the north end of Crewe station. Trains continuing southwards were only possible by shunting through a double siding. The M&BR became part of the LNWR in 1846.

Numerous stations were opened between Crewe and Manchester, today a popular commuter area. The first station northwards from Sandbach was (and still is) Holmes Chapel which at one time served an area with just a church and a few cottages in a wood. Today, close to the M6, the area includes a shopping precinct not far from now-demolished Saltersford

An early picture of Chelford station on the Crewe/Manchester line. In 1894 a serious accident at Chelford caused the loss of 14 lives. (Lens of Sutton)

Hall. There are tales that in earlier times salt was smuggled across the river Dane in coffins to avoid taxes, hence the name Saltersford.

The next station was Goostrey where the transfer of a stone commemorating the construction of Holmes Chapel and Stockport viaducts has, more recently, caused problems. It was transferred to the Brookside Garden Centre at Poynton with the blessing of Regional Railways North West but this action upset the local parish council.

Between Goostrey and Chelford, trains pass Jodrell Bank where in 1956 Professor Lovell established the world's largest radio telescope. When in 1842 the railway came to Chelford, the heart of the village had to move half a mile to the west, principally because the landowner of the Astle estate had refused permission for trains to cross his land. In 1894 there was a tragic accident at Chelford when an express train travelling at 60 mph collided with a wagon which was being shunted. Fourteen people died and a marble cross in the churchyard records this event. Before the First World War the approach to Chelford

Alderley Edge, south of Wilmslow, before the days of motor cars. Queen's Hotel is in the background. (Lens of Sutton)

station would be crowded each morning with horses and milk floats waiting for a special milk train.

The railway brought prosperity to Alderley Edge with Manchester businessmen, mostly cotton merchants, building many houses in the area. Owners of the houses were rewarded with silver medallions (worn on watch chains) which for a number of years entitled them to first class travel to and from Manchester.

Wilmslow station would at one time have seen steam expresses running between Manchester London Road (now Piccadilly) and the West of England. The station acquired junction status in 1909 when the Styal Loop was opened. This was built by the LNWR to meet a challenge from the Midland Railway which in 1902 added a further approach to Manchester from New Mills. The LNWR line provided a very direct route

Horse-drawn cabs wait for passengers at Wilmslow station. On the left are trucks from Poynton & Worth Collieries. (Lens of Sutton)

between Wilmslow and Manchester London Road, opening to passenger services on 1st May 1909. Stations were opened at Styal, Heald Green, Gatley, East Didsbury and Mauldeth Road. Burnage followed in July 1910. Euston services were transferred to what became known as 'the Styal line' (and sometimes still is) but they returned to the earlier route via Stockport in 1939.

On 'grouping' in the 1920s, the LNWR became part of the LMS network. Nationalisation followed in 1948 and electrification of the route was completed in 1961. Currently services from Manchester via Stockport include frequent electric DVT (driving van trailer) services to London Euston plus one diesel-hauled train daily cross country to Bournemouth.

Following the opening of a branch to Manchester Airport on 17th May 1993, the Styal line became better known to some as 'the Airport line'. The airport branch involved the construction of a new electrified double track some 1½ miles in length branching off the Styal line just south of Heald Green station. Manchester

Airport is currently the third largest in the UK, handling 13 million passengers annually. With the possibility of a second runway the number using the airport is predicted to rise to some 30 million annually by the year 2005. The rail link, comprising 158 DMU Sprinters or 323 EMUs, currently carries 1 million passengers a year.

The airport station was built to a futuristic design and comprised three levels. The upper level concourse links to terminals A and B. Lifts, escalators, ramps and stairs ensure ease of movement for passengers with luggage trolleys giving an effective passage from plane to train. Each side of the symmetrical island platform can accommodate trains of up to eight coaches in length. A southern spur has since been opened allowing hourly services from the airport to Wilmslow or Crewe.

5
Lines Around Macclesfield

Macclesfield/Cheadle Hulme/Manchester
Macclesfield/Kidsgrove/Stoke
North Rode/Leek/Uttoxeter
Congleton/Biddulph/Stoke
Macclesfield/Bollington/Marple

Cheadle Hulme c1910. Trains bore left for Macclesfield and right for Crewe. The Macclesfield branch was also used to carry coal from the pits at Poynton. (Lens of Sutton)

Macclesfield/Cheadle Hulme/ Manchester

Before the railways came, residents of Macclesfield had to rely on coach transport to Chelford to connect with the Manchester &

Macclesfield station was rebuilt in 1967 following electrification. Trains first reached Macclesfield in 1845 when the Cheadle Hulme branch opened. The original terminus was at Beech Bridge and a tunnel was needed to reach NSR tracks, which came in 1849. (Lens of Sutton)

Birmingham Railway (M&BR), which opened between Crewe and Manchester in 1842. The first trains to reach Macclesfield came from a junction with the M&BR at Cheadle Hulme on 24th November 1845. There was opposition in Macclesfield to the building of the line because the terminus was outside the town at Beech Bridge. A short tunnel was needed to reach the town centre but this was not completed until North Staffordshire Railway (NSR) trains reached Macclesfield from Congleton in June 1849. The NSR terminus was at Hibel Road and the M&BR trains (LNWR from 1846) were extended to that station.

The Cheadle Hulme to Macclesfield branch was also used to carry coal from pits at Poynton where a spur had been built to the collieries. It was considered that the first passenger station at Poynton, built where the track today crosses the A523, was too far from the village so this was closed in 1887 and another opened ¾ mile to the north.

Macclesfield station was rebuilt following electrification in

Stoke-on-Trent station in the late 1920s. Apart from being the North Staffordshire Railways (NSR) headquarters, the area also accommodated a large locomotive building and repair centre. (Lens of Sutton)

1967 and remains very much in use with most Euston-Manchester trains using the line via Stoke-on-Trent rather than operating through Crewe. Long since gone are the days when steam trains such as the 'Pines Express' would pass through the station. In the 1950s the former Hibel Road station was used as a locomotive depot with an allocation of a dozen or so engines. Sadly this depot has also gone and the site cleared. Macclesfield today has one station and one through line.

Macclesfield/Kidsgrove/Stoke

There were many problems when the NSR line was built from Stoke to Macclesfield via Congleton. Bad weather and shortage of cash hampered the construction of tunnels and viaducts. At Harecastle three tunnels were needed, 130 yds, 180 yds and 1,750 yds respectively in length to be separated by deep cuttings.

Stoke station square in earlier times. NSR trains first came to Stoke in April 1848 when a temporary station opened providing a service to Norton Bridge, giving a link with Birmingham and London. (Photograph courtesy City Central Library, Hanley)

Near Congleton two high viaducts had to be built, the longest being 1,255 ft with 20 spans and a height of 106 ft. The foundation stone was laid by the Mayor of Congleton on 25th September 1839 but construction costs proved prohibitive. During their work, the contractors had to avoid obstructing the Macclesfield Canal and were committed to a penalty of £5 per hour should this happen, the penalty to be doubled after 72 hours. NSR trains eventually reached Macclesfield on 18th June 1849 but only after further problems when piers at Congleton had to be rebuilt on rock bases following subsidence.

In October 1944 Harecastle station was renamed Kidsgrove Central and in 1964 it became just Kidsgrove. When the main line between the North West and Euston was electrified a diversionary line was opened on 27th June 1966 at Kidsgrove. This involved abandonment of Harecastle's three tunnels (see chapter 3).

Looking northwards at Harecastle station. Trains for Crewe and Sandbach branched left while main line traffic bore right towards Macclesfield and Manchester. Today the station is no more, with nearby Kidsgrove built at a new site. (Lens of Sutton)

While electrification of the main line between Euston and the North West was being completed in 1966/67, a diversion line was opened bypassing Harecastle's earlier three tunnels. This former tunnel, photographed in 1967, has now been demolished. (Courtesy Staffordshire County Museum, Shugborough)

Leek station, looking northwards, after closure to passengers in 1965. Freight traffic continued until final closure in 1970. The station has been demolished and the section infilled but the tunnel has survived. (Lens of Sutton)

North Rode/Leek/Uttoxeter

On 13th July 1849 the NSR began services from Uttoxeter via Leek on the Churnet Valley branch to join the Harecastle to Macclesfield line at North Rode. There were initially four trains each way daily with two on Sundays but equally important was the branch's freight traffic. Milk from the Churnet, Dane and Dove areas left regularly for London or Manchester. The branch could well have achieved far greater importance for it provided the shortest distance between Euston and Manchester. Although used by some through services, most of the trains ran via Stoke or Crewe.

Travelling southwards from North Rode, the line passed through pleasant countryside to reach Bosley, a timber-style station set in a cutting. Next came Rushton where the station building survives today as an attractive private residence. A prominent notice on the wall reads BEWARE OF TRAINS. Rudyard Lake station (opened in 1905) came next, known as

Cliffe Park from 1926. The lake was created as a reservoir for the Caldon Canal and it was at this lakeside that Stoke architect Kipling proposed to Rudyard Kipling's mother. The lake also later gave the famous novelist and poet his name.

At the south end of the lake came Rudyard (Horton) station which was known as Rudyard Lake prior to 1905. It seems hard to believe that not too many years ago on bank holidays, trains ran from Leek to Rudyard and back every quarter of an hour. Leek was reached after crossing the river Churnet and passing through the 462 yd Leek Tunnel. Today all trace of the station has gone and the site is occupied by a supermarket.

The North Rode to Leek section closed to passengers in November 1960 and Leek to Uttoxeter followed in January 1965. Freight continued for a time but in November 1992 even the lines which still exist from Stoke via Leek Brook junction to Oakamoor and Caldon Low were no longer in use.

Cheddleton station, sited some way from the village of the same name, possessed a small siding hardly adequate to cope with the output of a nearby paper mill. Yet today this area is put to good use by the Churnet Valley Railway Steam Centre. When visited recently by the author, all was activity. LMS class 4F 0-6-0 no 4422, rescued from the Barry Scrapyard in 1977, was in full steam hauling two coaches carrying many visitors. The engine had served much of its time in the south-west including a period in the 1950s on the much-loved former Somerset and Dorset line. The future for the Churnet Valley Railway looks good. The purchase of former BR track means passenger services between Cheddleton and Leekbrook. Further plans involve running trains southwards to Oakamoor Sand Quarry. It was a great boost for fundraising when in 1996 a full scale replica of Stephenson's *Rocket* was driven from Leekbrook to Cheddleton. This was the first steam train on that section of track for 30 years.

Congleton/Biddulph/Stoke

Another NSR branch, the Biddulph Valley line, reached a terminal at Congleton and by means of a spur was able to join

Congleton station, neo-Tudor in style with its decorative brickwork, stone dressings and patterned roof tiles. The station was completely rebuilt for the electrification scheme completed in 1967. (Lens of Sutton)

the Stoke to Macclesfield line. Since the movement of coal was the line's greatest priority, it commenced initially for goods only on 29th August 1860. Passenger services began on 1st June 1864, when the *Macclesfield Courier* reported, 'The first passenger train left Stoke at 8.45 am, the engine driver having decorated his iron horse with oak and laburnum, interspersed with a few flags emblazoned with the Staffordshire Knot.'

When the London, Midland & Scottish Railway (LMS) took over after grouping in the early 1920s, the Biddulph branch was one of the first to suffer. The LMS thought the line had no future for passenger traffic and regular Stoke/Congleton services ended on 11th July 1927. Mineral traffic continued healthily for many years even though the industry was in decline. In 1963 at Congleton the branch lost its spur to the main line with all goods traffic ending the following year.

Macclesfield/Bollington/Marple

A third railway reached Macclesfield on 2nd August 1869 when the Macclesfield, Bollington & Marple Railway (MB&M) opened a 10½ mile route from Marple Wharf junction (on the Sheffield & Midland Joint line) to a temporary terminus in Macclesfield.

An MB&M Act of 1864 empowered the NSR and the Manchester, Sheffield & Lincolnshire Railway (MS&LR) to subscribe £80,000 and to be responsible for the line's running and maintenance. Construction of the line was slow, despite only one major engineering work, a 23-arch viaduct near Bollington. Initially only single track was built and eventually on 2nd August 1869 the line opened to passengers. Freight traffic followed in March 1870.

One of the MB&M's objectives in building the line had been to provide a route to Manchester independent of the LNWR. Yet this was not to be since, after negotiations with the LNWR, a connecting link was built to join the MB&M with LNWR tracks.

Passengers await a train at Bollington station. The GC/NS Joint line opened to passengers in August 1869. (Lens of Sutton)

55

Middlewood station, between Macclesfield and Marple Rose Hill. The line closed in January 1970. (Lens of Sutton)

Despite the possibilities of through passenger services, it was only ever used for freight.

There were four intermediate stations between Macclesfield and Rose Hill junction. These were Bollington, Poynton (Higher Poynton from 1930), High Lane and Rose Hill, Marple. A station opened at Middlewood High Level (above the LNWR Middlewood) in 1879 and closed in November 1960. At Bollington a number of cotton mills existed but the line's main source of income was from the Poynton Collieries where a siding from Higher Poynton connected with the pits.

In 1871 an Act dissolved the MB&M, vesting the company in the NSR and the MS&LR (later the Great Central Railway) to become known as the Macclesfield Committee. Two years later, in 1873, the line was doubled and in 1886 a spur was built at the northern end of the line close to Middlewood station which allowed trains to reach Buxton. Apart from the regular services that began between Stoke and Buxton (via Macclesfield), the link also made possible a through London/Buxton service in competition with the Midland Railway although this was never much used.

The line between Macclesfield and Rose Hill closed to all traffic on 5th January 1970 although the short section from Rose Hill Marple and Marple Wharf junction remains open for services to Manchester Piccadilly.

6
Cheshire Lines Committee

Altrincham/Stockport/Godley
Altrincham/Northwich/Mouldsworth/Helsby
Cuddington/Winsford & Over;
Mouldsworth/Chester Northgate

The Cheshire Lines Committee (CLC) played an important role in the development of rail routes across Cheshire. It had strong claims to be called Britain's premier joint line and it linked the majority of the thriving industrial centres of Cheshire and Lancashire. Yet the CLC never owned its own locomotives – it always borrowed from other companies.

Mouldsworth station on the former Cheshire Lines Committee (CLC) route from Chester. A spur from Mouldsworth connected with Helsby, giving CLC trains access to Birkenhead. (Lens of Sutton)

Chester Northgate station which opened in 1874 was a terminus for the Cheshire Lines as well as Great Central trains from Connah's Quay. (Lens of Sutton)

The CLC owes its existence to Edward (later Sir Edward) Watkin, pioneer of many railway schemes throughout the country including a dream of a tunnel under the English Channel! One of Edward Watkin's companies was the Manchester, Sheffield & Lincolnshire Railway (MS&LR) which jointly with the Great Northern Railway (GNR) set out to reach the areas west and south-west of Manchester, then London & North Western Railway (LNWR) territory. To achieve this the Stockport & Woodley Junction Railway (S&WJR) was formed with Watkin's support. It was agreed by Parliament in May 1860 and work began in September 1860 when an official ceremony took place. There is a recollection of this event in Stockport's Vernon Park Museum where a barrow and spade are in its possession. The barrow is wooden with a metal-rimmed wheel. A plaque inside it reads, 'Presented to James Marshall Esq., Chairman of the Stockport & Woodley Junction Railway Company on the occasion of the cutting of the first sod of the railway on the 29th day of September 1860'. The line's short stretch of just under three miles opened on 12th January 1863

Hale station, south of Altrincham. During the Second World War, the station had a reputation for flower baskets and polished benches and in the winter coal fires would warm waiting passengers. (Lens of Sutton)

with the MS&LR and the GNR empowered to work the line.

The Cheshire Midland Railway (CMR) was incorporated in June 1860, also with Watkin's support. The company built a line from Altrincham to Northwich which opened in two stages, completed by 1st January 1863. On 11th July 1861 the West Cheshire Railway (WCR) was allowed by Parliament to construct a line from Northwich to Helsby to connect with the Birkenhead Railway from Hooton (see chapter 9). Next came the Stockport, Timperley & Altrincham Junction Railway (ST&AJR), incorporated on 22nd July 1861 to connect with Altrincham and the LNWR Manchester to Liverpool line.

It now seemed appropriate for the parent companies to amalgamate. A GNR and MS&LR Joint Committee was formed which represented the numerous companies already operating or authorised but not yet opened. Support also came from the Midland Railway (MR) with the result that the three main companies, the GNR, MS&LR and the MR, became joint and equal owners of a newly formed Cheshire Lines Committee

Passengers await a Manchester bound train at Northwich. In earlier times Northwich became a busy railway centre with sheds handling many visiting locomotives. (Lens of Sutton)

(CLC). Unusually it did not have the word 'Railway' in its title although it was generally referred to as the Cheshire Lines Railway. It was controlled by nine members, three from each company, agreed by an Act of July 1865. The CLC gained full independence in 1867 through the Cheshire Lines Act.

On 1st June 1864, a line of nearly four miles opened between Garston and Brunswick. This was built by the Garston & Liverpool Railway, another company to become part of the CLC. On 1st December 1865, the ST&AJR began services between Stockport and Altrincham, giving access to Northwich. On 1st February 1866 a spur from Baguley reached Broadheath junction, west of Altrincham, which meant that CLC trains, by using LNWR metals, could reach Garston and then continue on CLC rails to Brunswick (for Liverpool). In the same year a branch opened from Woodley junction to Godley, connecting CLC services with the Great Central Railway (GCR) line from Sheffield to Manchester.

The WCR opened its line from Northwich to Helsby on 1st

A deserted Northwich station in August 1996. The locomotive sheds have gone and all track in the area has been removed. (Author)

September 1869 for goods and a year later, on 22nd June 1870, for passengers. By a further Act, the WCR opened a branch of just under seven miles on 1st July 1870 from Cuddington to Winsford & Over primarily to transport salt from the mines and works along the west bank of the river Weaver. On the same day a short freight line of approximately 1½ miles opened to Winnington near Northwich.

The section between Mouldsworth and Helsby enabled CLC goods trains to reach Birkenhead. There were two stations, Manley and Helsby & Alvanley. Manley closed in 1875 yet Helsby & Alvanley had a mixed career. It also closed in 1875 but re-opened in 1936 only to close again in 1944. It opened yet again in September 1963 to last less than four months when the line closed to passengers on 6th January 1964. The station had been in existence for 94 years yet it had been open for only 13 of them! In September 1991 the branch was abandoned although the station building survives in private use.

No CLC trains reached Chester until 2nd November 1874

Barrow for Tarvin between Mouldsworth and Chester Northgate, a line opened by the Chester & West Cheshire Junction Railway in November 1874. Barrow closed in June 1953. (Lens of Sutton)

when a line was opened by the Chester & West Cheshire Junction Railway (C&WCJR) between Mouldsworth and Chester Northgate. The line had been agreed by Parliament in 1865 but completion had been delayed through lack of funds. The branch crossed the main GWR & LNWR Joint line from Chester to Warrington near Mickle Trafford. A connection was built but it was never used.

When 'grouping' came under the 1921 Railway Act, four main railways were formed. These were the London, Midland & Scottish (LMS), London & North Eastern (LNER), Great Western (GWR) and the Southern (SR). Logically it would have seemed the CLC should become part of the LMS but it was already financially involved with the GNR and the GCR (formerly MS&LR) both of which became part of the LNER. Its third member, the Midland Railway, became part of the LMS. The problem was solved by letting the CLC retain its independence.

It was however necessary for the committee of management to

Cuddington station, August 1996. A short branch from Cuddington to Winsford & Over closed to passengers in 1931 and to freight in 1958. The trackbed became a walkway known as 'Whitegate Way'. (Author)

change on 'grouping', with six members appointed from the LNER and three from the LMS. But the CLC kept its independent control of operations, its route mileage totalled 143¼ and it had become the fifth largest railway in the UK. It was not until nationalisation in 1948 that the CLC finally gave up its independence to become part of the London Midland Region of British Railways.

During the Second World War traffic increased considerably on CLC lines, much of it connected with troops through the ports. To handle the increased volume additional sidings were added, many of these in the Liverpool or Manchester areas (see next chapter). Between Mouldsworth and Helsby tracks were upgraded to cater for heavy oil traffic from Ellesmere Port and shipping at Birkenhead Docks. Between Knutsford and Mobberley private sidings were provided linking with a Government petrol storage depot at Shaw Heath. At Mickle Trafford a new junction was opened in October 1942 connecting the CLC with

The Railway Station — Knutsford

Knutsford station c1910. Advertisements on the water tower read 'Kilverts Lard' and 'Blue Cross Teas'. CLC passenger services between Altrincham and Northwich began in January 1863. (Lens of Sutton)

the GWR/LMS Joint line to relieve other services into Birkenhead.

Northwich became one of the busiest traffic centres of the system and to cope with this running loops were added to relieve congestion. Sheds at Northwich saw many visiting locomotives. They closed to steam in 1968, although diesels visited Northwich until well into the 1980s. Today all track at the sheds has been removed although memories of the steam days live on with the formation in 1981 of the 8E Association which helps to keep the railway spirit alive. The group takes its name from the 8E shed code which was fixed to locomotives stabled at Northwich.

After the war, motor traffic increased so rail traffic declined. The first station to go was Mickle Trafford which closed in February 1951 with Barrow for Tarvin following two years later. The branch to Winsford & Over had enjoyed a chequered career, closing to passengers from 1874 to 1876 and then again from

MOBBERLEY. C.L.C.

An early picture of Mobberley station and its level crossing. This CLC line today provides regular trains between Chester and Manchester although many may prefer the quicker route via Warrington. (Lens of Sutton)

1888 to 1891. It closed yet again during the First World War in 1917 and re-opened in July 1920. In 1930 the CLC announced the branch would finally close to passengers provided a suitable bus service could be arranged. The local Urban District Council objected and threatened legal action. At a hearing, the council's case was rejected and closure went ahead on 1st January 1931.

Freight traffic to Winsford & Over ceased in 1958. Today the former branch has become a walkway known as 'Whitegate Way'. The 3½ mile length is open to horse riders and walkers alike, offering easy walking along its length. Only a few reminders recall the past. A load gauge is still at Whitegate station and, where a level crossing once existed, rails can just be determined set in wooden blocks. Towards Cuddington a trackside hut with a flat roof can be found.

Chester Northgate station closed to passengers on 6th October 1969; the site is today a sports centre. In order to switch Manchester trains into Chester General, track alterations had to be made at Mickle Trafford. At Knutsford the signalbox, although still part of the signalling system, is normally switched

Delamere Forest station remains popular today with visitors to the nearby forest area. The station building currently houses a cafe. (Lens of Sutton)

out and it was last regularly manned in March 1994. The present owners, Railtrack, applied for permission for this to be demolished but, fortunately for conservation, this was refused. The box was built in 1886 and is the only surviving example built by Cheshire Lines signalling contractor Stevens & Co.

Today two-coach 142 DMUs or 150 DMUs run regular services between Chester and Manchester Piccadilly. They are still well used, particularly during the summer months. Any passenger wishing to travel from Chester to Manchester may well use the faster route via Warrington covering first the former LMS/GWR joint track to join the former CLC Liverpool to Manchester line at Earlestown.

With uncertainty over privatisation and concern over the outcome of less busy lines, it is encouraging to hear of a hope for the future. In February 1930, twenty-seven years of service from Chester's electric tramcars came to an end. Yet there is reason to believe that light rail may one day return to Chester's streets. The possibility follows a proposal from the early 1990s for a £67 million tramway scheme which was not pursued. A busway is

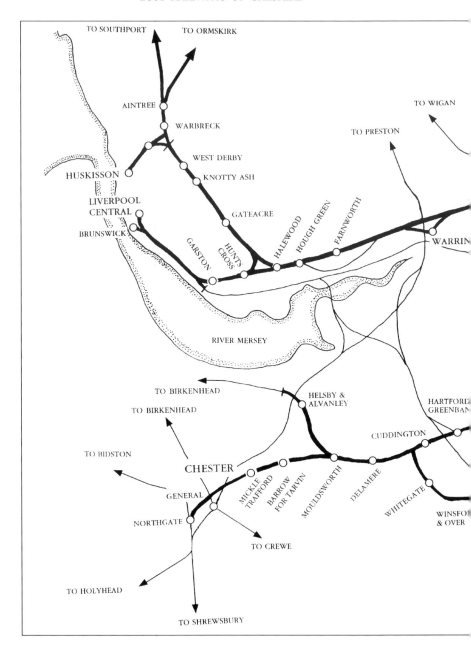

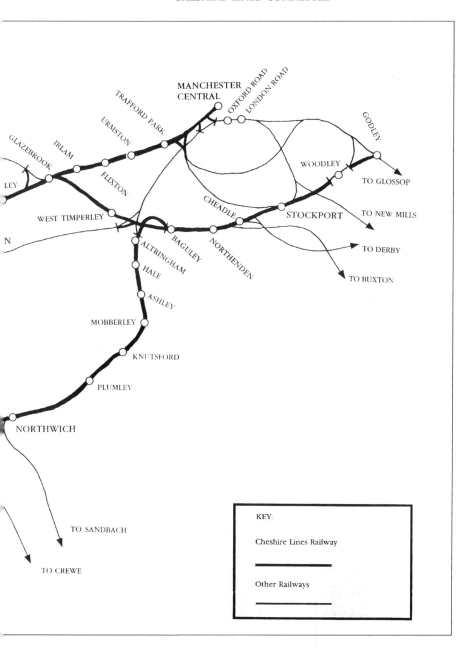

now being considered, putting to good use the redundant CLC railtrack from Mickle Trafford through Hoole and Newton to the former Chester Northgate area, thus linking with the city centre. Subsequent phases of development could include an extension to Blacon and Deeside and a further link to connect with the park & ride site (not yet built) on the A483 Wrexham Road to the south of the city. Guided busways require a specially designed concrete track and guideway, and small guide wheels fitted to the steering components under the front of a bus. This would give not only a smooth and quiet ride but also enable a bus to keep to a fixed track like a train. Although guided buses remain the current option, Cheshire County Council point out that such a busway could relatively easily convert to light rail usage.

7
Cheshire Lines Spread Northwards

*Liverpool/Warrington/Manchester
Glazebrook/Baguley; Halewood/Aintree/Southport*

Edward Watkin determined that the Cheshire Lines Committee (CLC) should build its own line to link Manchester and Liverpool. Previously any direct route had only been possible by using a line between Liverpool (Brunswick) and Garston and then reaching Manchester by using London and North Western Railway (LNWR) metals between Garston and Altrincham (Broadheath junction). The route was an arduous one with as

Glazebrook where tracks left the Liverpool/Manchester line to reach Baguley, giving through access from Liverpool to Stockport and beyond. (Lens of Sutton)

71

Urmston station c1908 on the CLC Liverpool to Manchester line which opened to passengers in 1873. (Lens of Sutton)

many as 95 level crossings along its length. Also relations with the LNWR were deteriorating, with the LNWR objecting to CLC trains along its tracks despite an earlier 'running powers' agreement.

Watkin therefore deposited a Bill on behalf of the Manchester, Sheffield & Lincolnshire Railway (MS&LR) to link Old Trafford (just outside Manchester) with a junction near Cressington on the existing CLC Garston to Liverpool Brunswick route. In addition he proposed to link Glazebrook with Baguley to give through access from Liverpool to Stockport and beyond. Thanks to backing from the Midland Railway (MR) and the Great Northern Railway (GNR) his proposals were agreed. But the support was more for the MR's and GNR's own political ends since supporting Watkin's plans strengthened their own positions in Lancashire against encroachment from rival companies. Parliament agreed Watkin's proposal in 1865 and work on the two lines began without delay despite opposition from numerous landowners. There were also problems with bad weather and with labour shortages in addition to continuing financial problems. Passenger services began eight years later in 1873.

A local steam train approaches Flixton station. Parliament agreed the Liverpool/Manchester line in 1865 but because of bad weather and financial problems it took eight years to build. (Lens of Sutton)

It was originally planned by the Act that a station would be built at Warrington to the north of the town on what became known as the 'straight line'. There was an immediate outcry about this from Warrington's citizens with the result a loop line between Sankey and Padgate junctions was proposed by an Act of 1866. The loop opened in March 1873 with Warrington station built midway, more in the town centre. The 'straight line' opened for traffic ten years later in August 1883.

Although Watkin now had his own line from Manchester to Liverpool, trains still only reached as far as Brunswick which was 1½ miles short of Liverpool Central station. Travellers had to be content with horse-buses which carried them to the CLC offices in James Street. The Liverpool Central Station Railway Act was agreed in July 1864 but it was to take the CLC another ten years before Central station was reached. In addition to financial troubles, it was also necessary to cut through rock, requiring four short tunnels. Trains eventually reached Liverpool Central station ten years later, on 1st March 1874.

Warrington Central station, August 1996. The station was originally planned to the north of the town but an outcry from local citizens produced a station close to the town centre. (Author)

Liverpool's Brunswick shed became an important depot even though cramped between the river and the railway at the end of Dingle tunnel (1,082 yds). Brunswick's shed became known as the Black Hole of Calcutta with engine smoke blowing back into the shed when the wind was in the wrong direction. Dingle tunnel also had its problems. The CLC had one of its few accidents in 1911 when a Manchester express ran into the rear of a Midland express. Eleven people lost their lives.

Watkin had achieved his objectives so far, linking Liverpool with Manchester and Stockport, and his trains had now reached Chester. However, the new main line from Liverpool to Manchester was restricted by inadequate facilities at its Manchester Oxford Road terminus and a new large and more central station was built. This opened in July 1877 but only as a temporary arrangement since in 1875 Parliament had approved a more permanent station. This was Manchester Central station which opened on 1st July 1880.

Drinking fountains were popular at CLC stations. This one is no longer in working order but it has been kept in reasonably good condition. (Author)

Further lines followed to complete the Cheshire Lines which served the county and the surrounding area for many years. In 1879 the CLC spread northwards, reaching Aintree and its famous racecourse. The following year a spur reached Huskisson Dock. Northwards from Aintree, tracks of the Southport & Cheshire Lines Extension Railway (S&CLER) reached Lord Street station, Southport. Services began on 1st September 1884 worked by the Cheshire Lines even though the S&CLER retained its separate identity.

Despite the years of prosperity that were to follow, Watkin remained ambitious. Efforts to reach Birkenhead on CLC lines failed, it could only be reached via Helsby and the Birkenhead Joint and then from Hooton on the GWR/LNWR Joint (see chapter 9). The nearest Watkin got to Birkenhead was when the Mersey Railway (with its Birkenhead connections) built a low-level station beneath the CLC at Liverpool Central. Efforts to run CLC services on the Liverpool Overhead Railway (see chapter 10) to reach Liverpool's docks also failed.

Manchester's CLC terminus with its great arched roof was designed by Sir John Fowler on similar principles to St Pancras. It closed in 1969 and is currently used as the Greater Manchester Exhibition and Event Centre. (Author)

Central Station and Bold St.

Liverpool

Liverpool Central station, terminus and headquarters of the Cheshire Lines Committee. The station with its fine single span arched roof closed in 1972 and has been demolished. (Lens of Sutton)

The CLC ran many troop trains during the First World War, particularly in 1917 when the USA joined in the fighting. A large reception camp was set up close to Knotty Ash station on the Halewood to Aintree route, also at the nearby Stanley LNWR station. Many Americans passed through these camps during the remainder of the war.

The effect of 'grouping' on the CLC by way of the 1921 Act has already been covered in the previous chapter and it was not until the outbreak of the Second World War in 1939 that the company saw its greatest changes. Port traffic at Liverpool, Birkenhead and Manchester increased dramatically bringing the lines their heaviest usage yet. Important Government works were also established on CLC lines, including an Ordnance Depot not far from Warrington, with the result that a new station with sidings opened at Risley in April 1940 to serve the factory. An RAF Maintenance Unit opened at Burtonwood, also near Warrington (later transferred to the American Air Force). Troop and freight train traffic on CLC lines remained heavy during hostilities and to cater for this numerous additional sidings were provided.

A nearly deserted Padgate station between Warrington and Birchwood. Birchwood station has only recently opened to cater for Warrington New Town traffic. (Lens of Sutton)

Because of the area's importance to the war effort, many heavy and prolonged air attacks were experienced. Liverpool suffered very badly and more than once Liverpool Central had to be closed. During a heavy raid in 1941 all the rail connections through the dock area were destroyed with the exception of one line connecting with Brunswick. The goods station at Huskisson (Liverpool) also suffered. Heavily bombed in 1940 and again in 1941 the station was damaged and a large storage warehouse completely destroyed. Serious problems also arose when the nearby Leeds & Liverpool Canal was hit by a bomb causing cascades of flood water to devastate the station area. Manchester also had its share. In 1940 the station and a large goods warehouse suffered badly from high explosive and incendiary attacks.

The early 1950s saw the beginning of decline. In 1951 stations closed at Otterspool and Halewood, both on the Liverpool to Manchester line. Risley station (opened 1940) closed on 7th January 1952. On the same day the line from Aintree to Southport ended passenger services. More closures followed with the Glazebrook to Godley line via Stockport gone to passenger traffic by November 1964. The Warrington 'straight line' closed in 1967 with Manchester Central station following on 5th May 1969 to become first a car park. It was later resurrected as the Greater Manchester Exhibition and Event Centre.

Yet not all was loss. The line from Manchester Oxford Road carries a regular DMU service to Chester. The Manchester to Liverpool line continues to run but now services are from Manchester Piccadilly (London Road until 1958) to Liverpool Lime Street. Liverpool Central is today an Underground station. The original CLC station has been demolished and has become a shopping precinct. At Hunts Cross there is a connection with the Merseyrail system (see chapter 10) taking passengers on towards Southport. Garston is not only a station on Merseyrail's Northern Line but also a link by bus with Liverpool Airport. Between Padgate and Glazebrook a new station called Birchwood has opened to cater for Warrington New Town traffic.

8
Lost Branches Across Cheshire

Kidsgrove/Sandbach; Sandbach/Northwich, Alsager Road/Keele

NSR locomotive no 21 class B leaves Harecastle c1920. Originally built as a 2-4-0T in 1882 at Stoke, it was rebuilt a 2-4-2T in 1901. In 1925 the LMS renumbered the locomotive 1457. (Lens of Sutton)

Kidsgrove/Sandbach

Passenger services between Kidsgrove (Harecastle until 1944) and Wheelock & Sandbach (Sandbach Wheelock until 1923) commenced on 3rd July 1893 with intermediate stations at

Hassall Green on the Harecastle/Sandbach branch where the station building has become a private residence. The bridge beyond carries the M6 motorway. (Author)

Lawton and Hassall Green. Between Hassall Green and Wheelock a short siding carried freight to and from Malkin's Bank, the vast alkali works of Brunner Mond, a forerunner of ICI. The line was never of any importance providing just three trains each way daily and five on Saturdays.

This North Staffordshire Railway (NSR) line of 6½ miles must surely have been one of the country's shortest-lived passenger lines. The Act agreeing to the branch was passed by Parliament in 1846 but it was to be another 47 years before it opened throughout to passengers and then it lasted only 37 years. Had it developed further, it could have taken NSR trains closer to Liverpool but, as it was, it settled initially for goods traffic only from 1852, between Lawton junction (on the main Crewe/Stoke line) and Ettiley Heath, a goods depot just short of Sandbach (on the Crewe/Manchester route). When goods services reached Sandbach in 1866, the branch was seen as a useful means to take pressure off some of Crewe's freight traffic.

Wheelock station building has become a garage while the former platform and trackbed at a lower level are lost in undergrowth. (Author)

On 28th July 1930 passenger services on the branch came to an end. Shortly before the closure date a charter train travelled the line carrying rail enthusiasts with more passengers than had been on the route for many years. The line continued usefully carrying freight until the early 1970s as a 'Crewe avoiding route' after which time much of the former trackbed became a walkway.

Hassall Green's former station building exists as a private residence although rather overshadowed by the M6 motorway. Wheelock station building has become a garage found at the top end of the town whilst the former platform is lost in a wooded glade below.

Two useful contributions to preserved railways came from the branch. The signal box currently in use at the Churnet Valley Railway Steam Centre at Cheddleton came from Elton crossing at Sandbach and the signal box and crossing gates at Hassall Green found their way to Hadlow Road station museum in the Wirral Country Park, on the former Hooton to West Kirby branch.

All that is left of Wheelock station where track passed below the A534 Sandbach Road. The station closed to passengers in 1930 but the line survived until the 1970s as a freight 'Crewe avoiding' line. (Lens of Sutton)

Sandbach/Northwich

Unlike the previous NSR Harecastle/Sandbach branch, a mostly-single line northwards towards Northwich assumed greater importance. The LNWR line received Parliamentary approval in 1863 and opened in November 1867 for goods traffic in an area which anticipated much salt and industrial traffic. Passenger services began the following year, on 1st July 1868. Intermediate stations were at Cledford Bridge Halt, Middlewich and Billinge Green Halt. In the early 1920s services included trains (weekdays only) from Crewe via the branch to Northwich with some travelling on to Acton Bridge or Warrington. One train daily ran each way between London Euston and Manchester via Crewe, Middlewich and Knutsford.

Sandbach was a busy junction in LNWR days. Apart from handling through trains from Crewe to Manchester, it also provided direct services to Northwich and (by NSR trains) to Harecastle. (Lens of Sutton)

The line's freight potential increased when a spur was built at Northwich allowing oil trains to travel directly from the busy Ellesmere Port refineries to join the former CLC tracks and then take the Northwich/Sandbach branch to continue to Stoke and the Potteries. There were hopes at one stage that the Northwich/Sandbach/Kidsgrove route might prove useful as a Crewe avoiding line but this did not materialise following the closure of the Sandbach/Kidsgrove line.

Cledford Bridge Halt and Billinge Green Halt both closed in 1942 and the line closed completely for passengers on 4th January 1960. Goods traffic closure followed seven years later. The track, currently owned by Railtrack, still exists today for freight traffic. Middlewich station's platform edges have survived and they can still be seen from an overbridge on the busy A54.

Middlewich station on the former line between Sandbach and Northwich closed to passengers on 4th January 1960. The buildings have gone but the platform edges can still be determined. (Author)

Alsager Road/Keele

This NSR mineral line between Kidsgrove and Keele was one of several similar prospects approved by Parliament on 29th July 1864 to serve such busy collieries as Audley, Bignall Hill, Rookery and Jamage. Construction work was slow, particularly between Silverdale and Leycett, requiring the excavation of a deep cutting followed by a high embankment. This section was beset throughout with problems from flooding and mining subsidence and was abandoned when an alternative route between Honeywall and Leycett became available in 1870.

There were further problems when many colliery sidings proved sub-standard and it was to be quite a number of years before the Board of Trade approved the line for passenger traffic.

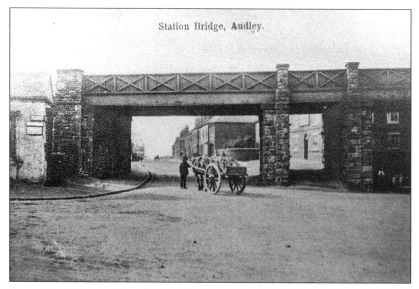

Station Bridge, Audley.

An early picture of Station Bridge at Audley. The station was originally known as Audley & Bignall End. Although primarily a mineral line, passenger services were provided lasting until 1931. Today only 'Bridge Close' indicates where the station existed. (Photograph by kind permission of the Borough Museum & Art Gallery, Newcastle-under-Lyme)

Eventually it was agreed the permanent way and the signalling met requirements and passenger services commenced on the Audley branch on 28th June 1880. There were four trains each way daily and two on Sundays. Intermediate stations were at Leycett, Halmerend and Audley with the buildings constructed of wood for cheapness. On 1st July 1889 a fourth station opened, called 'Talke & Alsager Road' but the name was shortened to Alsager Road in 1902.

During the period of depression after the First World War, many of the pits between Talke and Silverdale closed down. This stretch of track had for a time been among the most profitable on the NSR but as the pits became 'worked out' so hardship followed for the many men put out of work. When Talke pit closed in 1928, 1,000 men lost their jobs and in 1930 five more collieries closed down. On 27th April 1931 passenger services came to an end, finally forced to close by competition from buses which proved more convenient. Over the next three decades, freight services survived but they were run down as pits continued to close. In September 1957, Madeley Colliery at Leycett closed, the last of the once famous local pits, and by the late 1960s all freight had come to an end.

9
GWR/LNWR Joint Lines In The Wirral

Chester/Hooton/Birkenhead
Chester/Helsby/Warrington (Walton junction)
Hooton/Ellesmere Port/Helsby
Hooton/Neston/West Kirby

At its height Hooton station had seven platforms. It was an important junction on the Chester to Birkenhead line, serving also as starting points for branches to West Kirby and Helsby. (Author)

Chester/Hooton/Birkenhead

Early in the 19th century Birkenhead in the Wirral with its very

88

Despite its location close to the river Mersey, Port Sunlight station on the Chester/Birkenhead line, never gained any real importance. It started life as a workmen's halt. (Lens of Sutton)

small population was hardly known. But Liverpool lay directly across the Mersey and, since the 14th century, monks from Birkenhead Priory had been ferried across to what was then Lancashire. The monks considered they had an indefinite right to the ferry but such a situation could hardly last. A steamboat began making crossings in 1817 and within a year or so more were to follow. Many business folk in crowded Liverpool saw these ferries as a means to move out to the less congested Wirral.

By the time the Chester & Birkenhead Railway opened on 23rd September 1840 the town's population had reached 8,000. The line began as a single track from Chester to a terminus at Grange Lane (close to the ferries). It extended to a replacement terminus at Monk's Ferry in October 1844. Grange Lane station was replaced by Birkenhead Town but it was Birkenhead Woodside that became the eventual terminus in 1878. It had been intended that the station would directly connect with a landing stage for ferry passengers but ferry authorities were slow to act and when a large tram terminus was built in between, rail passengers had a longer walk to the boats.

Birkenhead Woodside which closed in 1967. Before the station was built, trains ran to Monks Ferry which later became a coaling point for steam-driven tugs. (Lens of Sutton)

Intermediate stations between Chester and Birkenhead opened at Bebington and Sutton (known as Ledsham from 1863), both with cottages used as platform buildings. Stations also opened at Hooton and Mollington with accommodation described as 'temporary'. Even at Chester a small wooden hut served as a booking office.

There is a tale from Ledsham from the early days of trains. An elderly stout gentleman was driven to the station each day by horse and trap – both rather decrepit. The driver was also very old and deaf. One day the gentleman climbed aboard and, as the trap moved forward, the floor gave way and the passenger found himself with his feet on the road and running like mad to keep up with the horse. The more he shouted the more the driver thought he was being urged to speed up to catch a train. It can only be presumed he arrived on time – perhaps a little breathless!

Amalgamation with the Birkenhead, Lancashire & Cheshire Junction Railway (BL&CJR) came in July 1847 when the line was doubled throughout. Further changes followed. In 1859 the company's title was simplified to become the Birkenhead Railway. The following year in October 1860 the Birkenhead Railway was absorbed into the Great Western and London & North Western Joint Railways (GWR/LNWR Joint).

There is no trace today of the original Grange Road, Birkenhead Town or Birkenhead Woodside stations. Woodside station became a car park. In 1891 Rock Ferry station (which opened in 1862) connected with Mersey Railway trains and in 1978 electric services reached southward to Hooton. A through electric service from Liverpool to Chester opened in August 1993 (see chapter 10). Travelling in these modern coaches, it is perhaps difficult to recall that this was once a single line track built well over 150 years ago to reach the ferries giving access to Liverpool.

Chester/Helsby/Warrington (Walton junction); Hooton/Ellesmere Port/Helsby

A BL&CJR line from Chester to Warrington opened to passengers on 18th December 1850 with intermediate stations at Dunham (later Dunham Hill) and Frodsham. Runcorn and Norton opened in the following year. Runcorn station was sited some three miles from the town, to be renamed Halton when the LNWR direct Liverpool line was opened in 1851 through Runcorn proper. Mickle Trafford came later in 1889. At Walton junction, just south of Warrington, BL&CJR tracks joined the existing LNWR (formerly Grand Junction Railway) line from Crewe.

Powers had originally been granted to the BL&CJR to build a 38½ mile line from Hooton (on the Chester & Birkenhead Railway) to Heaton Morris (on the Manchester & Birmingham Railway) crossing Grand Junction tracks at Keckwick (east of Runcorn). This would have had the advantage of linking Manchester's industrial districts with Birkenhead as well as provide a direct route between Manchester and Chester avoiding Crewe. The proposal upset the GJR which considered its existing

A LNWR 4-4-0 Benbow class locomotive with four coaches leaves Helsby station. The branch to the right connects with Birkenhead and Ellesmere Port. (Lens of Sutton)

Helsby station, August 1996, as a class 142 DMU leaves for Manchester Piccadilly. (Author)

92

HELSBY. 7/12/06

An 0-4-2T GWR class 517 locomotive derails at Helsby on 7th December 1906. The locomotive was built at Wolverhampton between 1868 and 1885 for light branch working. (Lens of Sutton)

lines were being duplicated. After negotiations the BL&CJR agreed to drop the section to Heaton Morris and instead joined the GJR tracks at Walton junction.

Helsby station opened in 1852, the only station today surviving between Chester and Frodsham. The town lies close to where many years ago quarrying on Helsby Hill was a thriving industry. Stones from the quarry helped in the construction of both Liverpool and Birkenhead Docks as well as many prominent buildings in Cheshire. It is said that the rocky escarpments of Helsby Hill (462 ft) have a strong resemblance to a man's face. Guide books quote, 'As long as Helsby wears a hood, the weather's never very good'.

A line from Hooton to Helsby opened on 1st July 1863 with intermediate stations at Sutton (Little Sutton from 1886), Whitby Locks (Ellesmere Port from 1870) and Ince (Ince & Elton from 1884).

Halton and Norton stations between Frodsham and Warring-

Frodsham station in busier times soon after the turn of the century. A LNWR 2-4-0 locomotive awaits departure while staff pose for a picture. (Lens of Sutton)

ton closed in 1952. A building survives at Norton (in private use) quite close to Runcorn East, a new station opened on 3rd October 1983 to serve the spread of homes from Runcorn itself. Frodsham station has survived the years, but on a visit in July 1996 there seemed very little information about train services – more apparent was scrawled writing telling us that 'Tracey loves Dave'!

Today class 150 DMUs run regularly between Ellesmere Port and Liverpool via Helsby, Warrington Bank Quay and Earlestown. Ellesmere Port also serves as a terminus for Merseyrail Electrics class 507 or 508 three or six car units travelling to Liverpool via Hooton. New stations opened at Stanlow & Thornton in October 1940 and at Overpool (between Little Sutton and Ellesmere Port) in August 1988.

A derelict and deserted unstaffed Frodsham station in August 1996. (Author)

Hooton/Neston/West Kirby

Visiting the Wirral Country Park today, it is all too easy to forget that trains once ran regularly from Hooton to West Kirby. The line closed to passenger traffic in 1956 and, after freight closure in 1962, the track was eventually lifted.

Fortunately a number of reminders still exist. The demand for future recreational needs in the Wirral with its increasing population prompted Cheshire County Council to purchase all possible land from British Rail and in this way the country park was born. Hadlow Road station was saved from demolition and restored to as it would have appeared in the 1950s. Here a visitor can find a ticket office with all the appearances of earlier days, milk churns, and posters from World War I. It seems that at one time three men worked at Hadlow Road, each sharing the surname Davies and whose Christian names were Tom, Dick and Harry! At Neston, a walking distance away, a rock cutting

Hadlow Road station on the former branch from Hooton to West Kirby. The station closed in November 1956 but today, as seen in this August 1996 picture, most of the station has been preserved. Much of the former trackbed has become a walkway and nature trail. (Author)

had been earmarked to become a rubbish tip but this too was saved. It now forms part of a popular nature trail.

A single track GW & LNW Joint Railway branch opened on 1st October 1866 to run along the Wirral's west coast. Initially trains from Hooton reached only as far as Parkgate which served as a terminus for almost 20 years. Parkgate was once famous as a port for steamers to Dublin as well as being a bathing resort. Also small collieries had existed along the shore and it was these various needs which led to the opening of the branch.

In April 1886 a new Parkgate station replaced the terminus and the line extended to West Kirby. Intermediate stations opened at Heswall and Thurstaston with Caldy and Kirby Park following later. At West Kirby the terminus lay adjacent to Wirral Railway tracks which carried trains through to Birkenhead. No through trains reached Birkenhead until 1923 when, following 'grouping', the London, Midland & Scottish Railway

Parkgate station was a single track terminus for 20 years until the branch from Hooton was extended to West Kirby in April 1886. (Lens of Sutton)

(LMS) acquired overall ownership and a service was introduced between New Brighton and Euston using the West Kirby branch.

Throughout its life the branch did what it could to attract customers. The 8 am train from Heswall provided a 'club' carriage with armchair seats and bridge tables for business men. Also local produce was not forgotten with farmers and fishermen making good use of the freight service available. The branch assisted in encouraging many commuters to live in the area.

In the 1950s the familiar decline of branch lines set in. The timetable suffered as a result and on 17th September 1956 passenger services came to an end. Six years later freight services were withdrawn and the branch had gone.

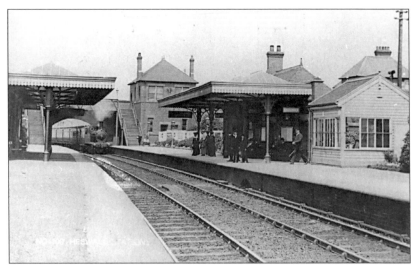

Heswall station c1910 on the Hooton to West Kirby branch. Heswall closed on 17th September 1956 and the area has been redeveloped. (Lens of Sutton)

Passengers leave a train at Heswall on the Birkenhead Joint railway. The train was hauled by a GWR 517 class 0-4-2T locomotive. (Lens of Sutton)

10
Electric Trains From Liverpool And A Tramway

Liverpool Central/Birkenhead Park; Liverpool/Rock Ferry
Birkenhead Park/Seacombe, New Brighton and West Kirby
Birkenhead Street Tramway

A railway tunnel under the river Mersey was opened by the Prince of Wales on 20th January 1886 and Mersey Railway trains between Liverpool's James Street and Green Lane at Tranmere commenced on February 1st 1886. Further services were soon to

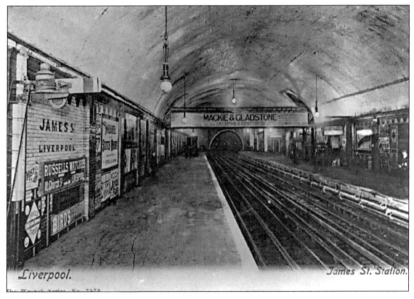

Liverpool's James Street station which opened in 1886. In steam days the Mersey Railway's underground stations were so dirty that traffic declined. The line was saved with electrification in 1903. (Lens of Sutton)

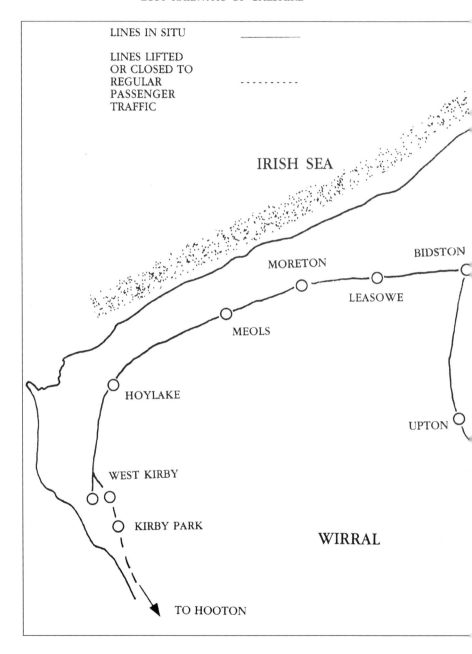

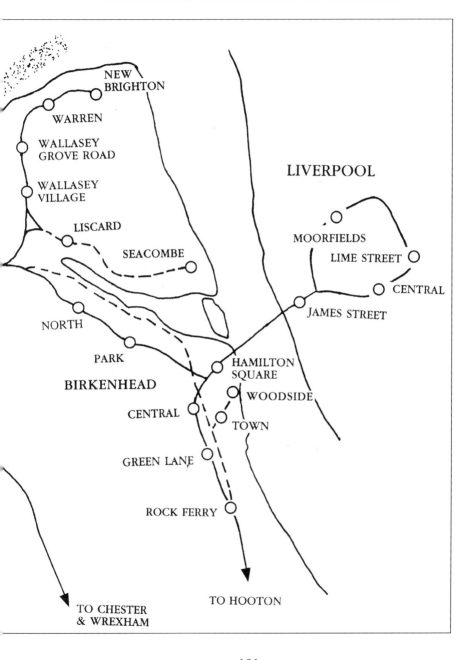

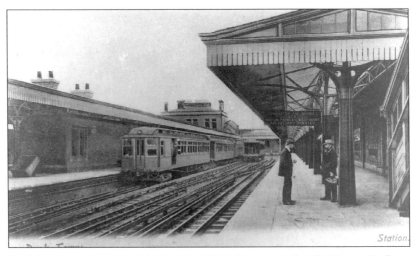

Rock Ferry station opened in October 1862. It connected with Mersey Railway trains in 1891 and, following electrification, extended south to Hooton in 1978. Through services reached Chester in 1993. (Lens of Sutton)

follow with a branch to Birkenhead Park opening on 2nd January 1888, extending to Rock Ferry on 15th June 1891. At Birkenhead Park there was an end-on junction with trains of the Seacombe, Hoylake & Deeside Railway which later became the Wirral Railway. An extension to a new low-level station under Liverpool Central followed on 11th January 1892 but this section presented difficulties with gradients taxing locomotives to their limits, one as steep as 1 in 27. There were problems too with smoke and foul air in the tunnel despite the installation of massive steam-driven ventilating fans. Some 10 million passengers a year used the railway but this number declined as conditions deteriorated with many transferring to the ferries.

Clearly action was needed so in 1900 the company got the go-ahead to electrify its railway system. Track was relaid, stations and tunnels were cleaned up and electric pumps and fans were installed. When the first electric trains began running on 3rd May 1903, the Mersey Railway had the distinction of being the first steam-worked railway to convert to an electric system. The company was not however the first to run electric trains. Liverpool's initial electric system opened in March 1893, this

Hamilton Square on the Mersey Railway. The station opened in January 1886 with steam-worked trains on a line that was the world's first under river railway. (Lens of Sutton)

being the first elevated line in the world. The trains ran through a dockland area with the track raised on girders, known locally as the 'Dockers' Umbrella'. The 'Liverpool Overhead' was also the first in Great Britain to introduce an automatic signalling system.

In 1934 the first road bridge under the Mersey was opened, yet the Mersey Railway (as it was originally known) remained the busiest commuter system outside London. Through working between Liverpool Central and New Brighton and West Kirby commenced on 13th March 1938 thus avoiding a previously necessary change at Birkenhead Park.

The Merseyrail system maintained its popularity over the years. Stations on the Wirral boasted frequent services to Liverpool. A hoarding at Birkenhead Hamilton Square in the 1950s read 'To Liverpool in Three Minutes'. Liverpool Central's low-level station closed in July 1975 and two years later in May 1977 a loop line opened serving trains from the Wirral, running clockwise from Liverpool's James Street to Central and continuing on back to James Street.

The Wirral Railway had its beginnings in the Hoylake Railway

Birkenhead. *Booking Hall, Hamilton Square Station.*

The booking hall at Hamilton Square station in Edwardian times. The line had the distinction of being the first steam-operated railway to convert to electric trains in the country. (Lens of Sutton)

which in 1863 had powers to construct a line from Hoylake to Seacombe and also to Birkenhead Docks. Further Acts were agreed in 1865 and 1866 respectively for a branch to New Brighton and an extension from Hoylake to Parkgate but initially only a 5¼ mile stretch from Hoylake to Birkenhead Docks was built. This opened on 2nd July 1866, but with much of the route undeveloped and Hoylake a mere fishing village, traffic was poor. In July 1870 it closed down when bailiffs seized the line. The line was re-opened in 1872 by the Hoylake & Birkenhead Rail & Tramway Company (H&BR&TCo) which also ran a street tramway to Woodside Ferry. This street tramway was sold to the Birkenhead Tramways in 1879.

Birkenhead's trams (the Birkenhead Street Railway Co Ltd) were introduced by (inappropriately) George Train. He came from America where 'street cars' had been introduced in New York in 1832. After failing to persuade the Mersey Docks to accept his ideas, he had better success at Birkenhead where construction began in June 1860. When the 1¼ mile tramway

104

Wirral Railway's locomotive 0-4-4T approaches Wallasey station. Wallasey was renamed Wallasey Grove Road in 1948. Trains first reached Wallasey from Birkenhead in 1888 encouraging much development as a residential area. (Lens of Sutton)

from Woodside Ferry to Birkenhead Park began on 30th August 1860, Train claimed it to be the 'first street railway in Europe'. The opening was a grand affair. All the crowned heads of Europe were invited (except for some unknown reason the King of Naples) and some 350 people were present to drink no fewer than 11 toasts!

But the wrought iron protruding step rails caused problems and these had to be replaced by grooved rails set flush with the road's surface. Two of the horse-drawn cars were 48-seaters and provision was made for straphanging – an innovation. Birkenhead's trams progressed in 1901 to an electric system, to finally close in 1937.

On 1st April 1878 the line at Hoylake was extended to West Kirby and in 1881 the company became known as the Seacombe, Hoylake & Deeside Railway (SH&DR). Seven years later, on 2nd January 1888, the Wirral Railway Company came into existence when a line was opened from Birkenhead Docks to Birkenhead Park to join the Mersey Railway at Hamilton Square. The same

Birkenhead Electric Tramways (1901-1937) seen here at the Laird Street terminus. Prior to electrification, horse-trams were used which until 1879 were owned by the Hoylake & Birkenhead Rail & Tramway Company. (Lens of Sutton)

day the SH&DR reached Wallasey, and New Brighton two months later. A branch to Seacombe opened on 1st June 1895.

In 1889 the GWR/LNWR Joint Railway made a bid to take over the SH&DR but this was rejected. Instead the SH&DR joined the Wirral Railway to form a new Wirral Railway. This was soon to become a busy commuter line with frequent services to and from each of its four terminal stations. Powers to electrify in 1900 (along with the Mersey Railway) were not taken up until Government financial backing came in 1935. Electric trains on the Wirral Railway came in March 1938 with services from Birkenhead Park to West Kirby and New Brighton running jointly with LMS and Mersey Railways. Traffic to Seacombe was always at a low level and closure appeared inevitable when it was excluded from the electrification programme. The end finally came on 4th January 1960 with the trackbed later used to provide the M53 with an approach to the second Mersey road tunnel, opened eleven years later in 1971.

Long since gone are the wooden electric coaches painted in BR

Staff pose at New Brighton station which opened in 1888. The line from Bidston to New Brighton was not electrified until March 1938. (Lens of Sutton)

This type of wooden stock painted in BR green, seen here at Birkenhead Central, lasted until 1956 when new coaches were introduced. Today class 507 or 508 units are seen on Mersey tracks. (Lens of Sutton)

green which were withdrawn in 1956. Today Merseyrail Electrics run regular class 507 or 508 three or six car units every 15 minutes during the day between New Brighton and via the Liverpool loop to West Kirby and back. Electric trains also run between Liverpool and Chester or Ellesmere Port.

11
Great Central Lines
In The Wirral

Chester Northgate/Hawarden Bridge
Bidston/Hawarden Bridge/Wrexham

Hawarden Bridge across the river Dee opened in August 1889 so that trains from the Wirral could connect with North Wales. The bridge required two girder spans and a hydraulically operated swing span. (Author)

Chester Northgate/Hawarden Bridge

In July 1884, as no trains yet crossed the river Dee between Hawarden and Shotton, the Manchester, Sheffield & Lincolnshire

Chester Northgate station in the 1960s. A poster by the entrance read 'London Shopping 60/- Day Return from Chester'. (Lens of Sutton)

Railway (MS&LR and known as Great Central Railway from August 1897) obtained Parliamentary powers to build a bridge so that trains from the Wirral could connect with North Wales. The bridge proved expensive, requiring two girder spans and a 287 ft hydraulically-operated swing span. It was opened amid celebrations in August 1889 by the wife of the Rt Hon W.E. Gladstone who lived at Hawarden Castle. On 31st March 1890 a service of four trains daily began between Chester Northgate and Wrexham via Hawarden Bridge. Connah's Quay docks increased in importance. Now approached from the Wirral as well as from North Wales it became well equipped for the rapid handling of traffic.

Intermediate stations on the line from Chester to Hawarden Bridge opened at Chester Liverpool Road, Blacon and Saughall as well as two small halts used solely by Chester Golf Club. Blacon and Saughall stations both had attractive black and white buildings typically late Victorian and similar to styles in Chester itself. During the First World War a halt near Saughall opened

110

Chester Northgate station closed to all traffic on 6th October 1969. The site is today the Northgate Arena Leisure Centre. (Author)

for military personnel only, serving Shotwick Park Aerodrome and Queensferry Acceptance Park. It opened to the public in 1919 and was renamed Sealand in 1931.

The Chester to Hawarden Bridge line survived for passenger traffic until 9th September 1968. Chester Northgate closed on 6th September 1969 and goods traffic was diverted to Chester General until 20th April 1984 when all traffic between Chester and Hawarden Bridge came to an end. In 1986 the line re-opened as single track for freight from Hawarden Bridge to Mickle Trafford (on the main Chester to Warrington line). Today this track is no longer in use but there are hopes that it will become part of a guided busway system (or even trams) linking with park & rides outside the city and later with the Deeside Industrial Park (see chapter 6). It could also connect with the Wrexham to Bidston line.

Bidston station, terminus for DMUs from Wrexham and a through station for Merseyrail Electrics between Liverpool and West Kirby, seen here in the 1960s. (Lens of Sutton)

Bidston/Hawarden Bridge/Wrexham

In today's world of the motor car and the many motorways that serve the county, it is perhaps surprising that the rail service from Wrexham to Bidston should have so far survived. Yet some 14 trains (DMUs) run daily on weekdays plus a limited service on Sundays. At Bidston, set in an isolated area in the north of the Wirral and close to the M53, travellers from North Wales can change to catch a Merseyrail electric train for Liverpool. But trains between Wrexham and Bidston must keep good time for only a few minutes are allowed for the change and the timetable states that 'connections cannot be guaranteed'.

The line down the centre of the Wirral peninsula was initially conceived by the first Wirral Railway as a branch to connect Birkenhead with the Chester & Connah's Quay Railway. This in turn was to cross the river Dee and meet the Wrexham, Mold &

112

Heswall station (formerly Heswall Hills) on the Bidston/Wrexham line appeared neglected when visited in August 1996. Weeds covered much of the trackbed and a cross-over had been only partly removed. (Author)

Connah's Quay Railway (WM&CQR) to connect with Wrexham.

The WM&CQR line had been constructed initially to carry mineral traffic from North Wales to the Dee and link with Cheshire's salt works so the possibility of a connection with Birkenhead was an attraction indeed. Numerous branches already existed north of Wrexham including lines to Gwersyllt Colliery, Ffrwd Ironworks, Brynmally Colliery and further coalfields at Brymbo.

In 1889 the MS&LR and the WM&CQR combined to form the Wirral Railways Committee and in 1895 this became known as the Dee & Birkenhead Committee. Freight traffic began on 16th March 1896 with passenger services following on 18th May 1896. The delay in opening was partly due to the Mersey Railway's refusal to allow trains other than its own through the Mersey tunnel into Liverpool, so Wrexham trains continued on Wirral Railway tracks to terminate at Seacombe instead. The line became known as the North Wales & Liverpool Railway but on

113

Wrexham Central station before closure of the line (seen on the right) to Ellesmere. In 1996 plans were announced to relocate the station to the west of its present site. (Lens of Sutton)

Burton Point station between Neston and Hawarden Bridge closed in December 1955. The platform edging and footbridge have long since been removed. (Author)

1st January 1905 it was absorbed by the Great Central Railway (GCR). On 'grouping' it became part of the London & North Eastern Railway (LNER), giving the company its only line into Wales.

South of Bidston stations opened at Upton, Storeton (for Barnston) and Neston & Parkgate (renamed Neston in 1968). Heswall Hills followed in May 1898 and Burton Point in August 1899. In July 1901 Seacombe became known as Seacombe & Egremont only to revert back to Seacombe in January 1953.

By the 1920s some twelve trains were running daily between Wrexham Central and Seacombe with the journey across the Mersey to Liverpool to be completed by ferry. At its peak, Wrexham claimed three busy railway stations. These were Wrexham Central for GCR Bidston services (also trains to Ellesmere), Wrexham General for GWR trains between Chester and Shrewsbury and also Wrexham Exchange where GCR and GWR trains met.

Efforts have been made in the past to close Wrexham Central but this has so far been successfully resisted due to its proximity

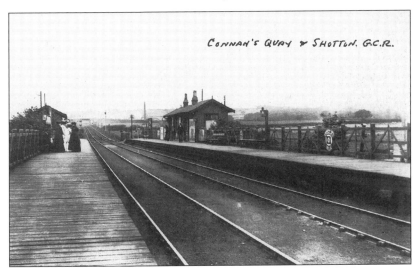

The GCR Connah's Quay & Shotton station south of the river Dee c1910. This view is taken looking southwards towards Buckley and Wrexham. (Lens of Sutton)

Connah's Quay & Shotton (renamed Shotton) in August 1996. Some 14 DMUs pass daily through the station between Wrexham and Bidston. (Author)

to the main shopping centre. Perhaps it is a sign that the Wrexham to Bidston line up the Wirral will survive closure since plans are in hand to relocate Wrexham Central station to the west of its present site. This follows proposals for a new purpose-built station, placing it adjacent to retail and leisure outlets.

At Wrexham General the architecture recalls the past but it is many years since crowds came by train to attend the nearby race meetings. The racecourse is the football pitch of today but the nearby Turf Hotel is still so named as a reminder of the past. Wrexham Exchange closed in June 1981 when it became linked to and renamed Wrexham General.

By the 1950s the motor car was taking over and stations were becoming redundant. Storeton closed in 1951 leaving no trace. Burton Point station went four years later although much of the platform building remains. In January 1960 Seacombe branch closed and Wrexham trains had to terminate at Bidston (as they do today). The former Seacombe branch became an approach

116

road to the second Mersey road tunnel (see chapter 10).

Between Wrexham and Hawarden Bridge numerous stations have survived. These include Buckley Junction station (renamed Buckley in 1974) which has been converted to industrial use although a small halt remains. Connah's Quay & Shotton station has been renamed Shotton. Two-coach DMUs may today provide a service between Wrexham Central and Bidston but it is many years since LNER class 13 Atlantic tanks hauled passenger trains as far north as Seacombe. In these days of 'rationalisation' and 'privatisation' one can only hope that a line such as this will continue.

As already recalled, the line between Bidston and Wrexham began passenger services on 18th May 1896. To remember this event, a special train was run from Hawarden to Liverpool Central Low Level via the Mersey Railway on 18th May 1996. This would not have been possible last century since the Mersey Railway refused to allow trains from Wrexham over its tracks.

The booking office and waiting room above the former Burton Point station remain virtually intact, today used by Station House Nursery. (Author)

117

12
A Trunk Route To Holyhead

Chester/Rhyl/Llandudno junction/Bangor/Holyhead

Had early railway planners had their way, then the line from Chester to Holyhead might never have materialised. In 1836 routes were surveyed through the Welsh mountains to Porth Dinllaen harbour in Caernarvon Bay. The Great Western Railway (GWR) considered a route from Gloucester to New Quay in Cardigan Bay. Both ideas failed, similarly a line from Chester to Ormes Bay (Llandudno) was considered yet never developed.

The Chester & Holyhead Railway (C&HR) was given Parliamentary approval in July 1844. The company had the

Ex-LMS 4-6-0 locomotive named 'E. Tootal Broadhurst' hauls coaches through Chester, travelling from Llandudno to London Euston on 20th June 1963. (D.K. Jones)

A diesel-hauled freight train approaches the Dee bridge in Chester from Saltney junction. To the south the line splits providing services either to Wrexham and Shrewsbury or westwards on the main Chester-Holyhead line. (Author)

support of the Grand Junction Railway and the London & Birmingham Railway. To allow construction to begin without delay, powers to cross the Menai Strait were deferred until the next session. But there were delays and work covering the first eight miles out of Chester did not begin until 1st March 1845 (St David's Day). The first objective was to reach Bangor and by mid-1846 some 12,000 men were at work.

The C&HR were good employers. They paid the men in cash every other week and there was no Sunday work except for those tunnelling which carried on 24 hours a day and seven days a week. Consideration was given also to the moral welfare of the workers. The company part financed the employment of six missionaries who were paid £60 a year to read and talk to the men during their meal breaks. The men, many living in squalid turf huts and most earning less than 5 shillings a day, often spent their money on drinking sessions yet quite a number listened to the missionaries. It was known for labourers to find money to buy bibles, cash they could scarcely afford.

The line from Chester to Saltney junction (1¾ miles) opened on 4th November 1846. Just over six months later, on 24th May 1847, an iron bridge over the river Dee collapsed and six people died (see chapter 13). Meantime construction of the Chester to Holyhead line had pushed ahead and a tubular bridge was built to cross the estuary at Conway. The tubes were completed on the shores of the estuary and then floated into position on pontoons and raised by hydraulic presses. Between Conway and Penmaenmawr, a towering headland made it impossible to follow the coastline. Efforts to cut an embankment out of the rock face gave problems through constant assaults by the sea and the danger of falling boulders from above. Penmaenbach tunnel (718 yds) was built with covered ways either side.

Services from Chester to Bangor began on 1st May 1848 with four trains each way daily and two on Sundays. An Act to build a railway bridge over the Strait had already been agreed in 1845 but Robert Stephenson, then C&HR engineer, had not then decided how to get trains across the water. It had been suggested that coaches could be hauled across Telford's suspension bridge (completed 1826) by rope or a horse. Stephenson eventually decided to construct a bridge comprising tubular beams with trains running inside. The beams would be supported by towers.

Work on Britannia Bridge began in 1846 and, as at Conway, the tubes were manufactured from wrought iron, then floated into position on pontoons. Hydraulic presses raised them onto stone bridge towers. There was a moment of panic when one press failed and one tube dropped but fortunately support had been provided beneath. The bridge was completed in 1850 and when Stephenson drove the first locomotive across, cannons were fired in celebration. First through trains from Chester to Holyhead began on 18th March 1850.

The railway company considered all possible comforts for the passengers. Travellers were advised to take as little luggage as possible and never to open carriage doors themselves. No dogs were permitted in the carriages and smoking was not allowed. If travelling in darkness the company recommended the purchase of a railway lamp. To avoid vibration when reading a book,

Llandudno junction station in steam days. Through trains from Chester to Holyhead began in March 1850 and in 1858 a three mile branch to Llandudno town opened to cope with increasing seaside excursion traffic. (Lens of Sutton)

passengers were told that elbows should not be rested on any solid part of the carriage – 'books should be held in both hands and supported by muscular power'.

Despite the expected tourist boom, the C&HR was never financially sound. Locomotives and rolling stock had to be provided by the London & North Western Railway (LNWR) and by early 1859 the LNWR was compelled to take over the smaller company's debts and liabilities.

By the end of the last century, the seaside towns along the route were gaining in popularity and track layouts were improved. Work was also undertaken to provide four tracks instead of two along much of the route to cope with the extra trains required. Freight traffic also proved profitable with mineral works developing along the Dee Estuary, adding to the existing goods traffic from Ireland. There was also considerable movement of coal which was taken to the steamers at Holyhead.

Llandudno steadily increased in importance, becoming a 'much frequented bathing and watering place'. In October 1858

Ex-LMS 4-6-0 locomotive no 45427 hauls a Liverpool-Holyhead train close to Saltney junction on 20th July 1963. The engine running light is a standard LMS 0-6-0 class 4F. This cutting was a favourite spot for train-spotters in steam days. (D.K. Jones)

a three mile branch opened from the main line into Llandudno town. Soon many excursions were arriving at the resort and staff had to be increased to cope with the extra traffic. An intermediate station at Deganwy opened in 1866. By 1885 some 28 trains were arriving daily at Llandudno with through coaches from London, the Midlands and Lancashire. In addition there were many excursions.

During the latter part of the 19th century there were many achievements along the main line. The 'Irish Mail' could cover the 84½ miles between Chester and Holyhead in just over two hours. Troughs and scoops were introduced by LNWR locomotive superintendent James Ramsbottom so that tenders could pick up water at speed, allowing non-stop expresses. They lasted until the late 1960s. Eight-wheeled coaches came in 1883 and proper sleeping cars from 1891. The latter were equipped with the luxury of a lavatory at either end. Well-to-do passengers could buy lunch baskets at Chester. Five shillings could purchase a pint of claret or half pint of sherry together with chicken, ham

Sandycroft, between Saltney junction and Shotton, which closed on 1st May 1961. Note the extravagant booking office at street level. (Lens of Sutton)

or tongue and bread, butter and cheese.

During the 1880s businessmen's trains began daily between Manchester and Llandudno, with 'club' coaches providing special saloon accommodation following in 1908. There were frequent visits too from North Staffordshire Railway trains operating express services from the Potteries. During the First World War Holyhead became a destroyer base thus increasing goods traffic. Other routes to Ireland closed due to activity from enemy submarines and several railway steamers were lost. During the 1930s holiday traffic became even busier. Royal Scot 4-6-0s took on the mail trains. When a holiday camp opened at Prestatyn in 1939 passenger traffic reached its maximum.

In the 1950s Princess Coronation Pacifics and Britannias took over and a road bridge across the tracks near Saltney proved a popular vantage point for train-spotters. In the mid-1960s local passenger services gave way to diesel multiple unit (DMU) working. But increasing motor traffic was forcing closure of many of the smaller stations. Sandycroft went in 1961 and others which followed in 1966 included Queensferry, Shotton, Connah's Quay and Bagillt. Shotton re-opened in 1972 to passengers.

The former Connah's Quay station looking towards Flint. The station closed on 14th February 1966. (Lens of Sutton)

Saturday, 23rd May 1970 proved a disastrous day for the Britannia Bridge which carried trains across the Menai Strait. It was reported that boys looking for birds' nests in one of the tubes lit a paper torch and then dropped it by mistake. It fell among rubbish and the resultant fire, fanned by air currents, spread along the roof from one end to the other. The wrought iron tubes eventually sagged with the great heat generated, tearing their tops where they passed through the towers. All traffic was suspended and various locomotives, multiple units and rolling had to be recovered from Anglesey by road.

The bridge was immediately redesigned with the towers remaining but the tubular tubes idea abandoned. Instead a steel arch construction was built with two main spans and steel members, also with supporting piers for the approach spans. The steel arches were completed by the end on 1971 and the first train, a special DMU from Chester crossed the bridge on 30th January 1972. During construction, consideration had been given to adding a road bridge above the railway and this was built between 1977 and 1980.

Today tourists still visit the many resorts along the route but it

124

Shotton station on the main Chester/Holyhead line looking towards Flint. A high-level Shotton station serves trains on the Bidston/Wrexham line. (Author)

Rhyl station c1910. Before the days of the motor car, this station was kept very busy with seaside holiday traffic. (Lens of Sutton)

is not usual for trains to take them there. Sadly, too, the bulk of the freight along the coastline is no longer hauled by rail. Instead it is carried on roads hardly adequate to cope with the extra loads.

13
The Shrewsbury & Chester Railway

Chester/Wrexham/Shrewsbury

The Shrewsbury and Chester Railway (S&CR) came into existence following the consolidation of two companies, the North Wales Mineral Railway (NWMR) and the Shrewsbury, Oswestry & Chester Junction Railway (SO&CJR) in July 1846. On

Chester's Dee railway bridge which in May 1847 collapsed as a Ruabon train crossed, causing many coaches to fall in the river below. Five people were killed in the accident. The bridge today carries just two tracks with redundant trackbeds to the left. (Author)

Chester station today retains much of its earlier architecture. The station opened in August 1848, designed by Francis Thompson and constructed by Thomas Brassey. (Author)

4th November 1846 the NWMR section opened from a temporary station at Chester to Ruabon. There were five trains each way daily with two on Sundays. The coaches were considered a luxury since the second-class carriages had partitioned compartments and glass windows. Between Chester and Saltney junction, S&CR trains ran on Chester & Holyhead Railway (C&HR) metals. Main intermediate stations between Chester and Ruabon opened at Saltney, Rossett, Gresford and Wrexham.

On 24th May 1847 there was a terrible railway accident, long remembered locally. As the 6.15 pm from Chester to Ruabon approached Dee bridge close to the Roodee racecourse, the driver felt 'a kind of vibratory noise in the girders'. He accelerated, hoping to clear the bridge, but hardly had the engine and tender reached the other side when two of the bridge's girders gave way. There was a tremendous crash and carriages were thrown onto the embankment below, many

Chester station in today's diminished state. In earlier times it was completely covered by an iron and glass roof. The station area included carriage and goods sheds. (Author)

rolling into the river. The *Chester Courant* reported, 'The screams of the wounded and the groans of those whose limbs were broken were heartrending. Strong iron chains were snapped and one carriage was crushed like a nut shell by the fall.' Five people were killed.

The collapse came as quite a setback for Robert Stephenson who had designed the bridge. It came at a time when people needed to be convinced that the railways were safe. Yet the accident was also remarkable for the courage shown by the driver of the engine. He immediately drove minus his tender to Saltney junction where he gave the alarm, then crossed to the down road to re-cross the bridge by the remaining girders to warn up traffic and summon help from Chester. For some two months following the accident, rail passengers had to finish their journeys to Chester by horse-bus until the bridge re-opened on 26th July 1847.

A joint station at Chester shared by the S&CR and the C&HR

Wrexham General station in steam days. At one time Wrexham had a third station, Wrexham Exchange, on the Bidston line. It closed in June 1981 to become part of and linked to Wrexham General. (Lens of Sutton)

opened on 1st August 1848. Designed by Francis Thompson and constructed by Thomas Brassey, it had a fine 1,050 ft frontage and it was completely covered by an iron and glass roof. The station area included a large carriage shed, a large goods shed and a triangular junction used for turning locomotives.

Building the section from Ruabon to Shrewsbury involved considerable engineering works since it was necessary to cross the Dee and Ceiriog valleys. At the latter near Chirk a long stone and timber viaduct was built (replaced by masonry arches in 1858/9). The S&CR engineer, Henry Robertson, was congratulated on such 'a magnificent achievement' by the Board of Trade Inspector Captain Wynne who inspected the line prior to opening. But the Inspector added the comment that the Ceiriog viaduct, built alongside and above Telford's canal aqueduct, 'completely degraded the other which had for so long given celebrity to the valley'.

When the Ruabon to Shrewsbury section opened on 12th October 1848, there were great celebrations. Crowds turned out for the opening at railway stations along the line to wave and

Rossett station on the Chester/Shrewsbury line served a busy community. It closed in October 1964 but survived as a goods depot for a further four years. (Lens of Sutton)

cheer. The inaugural train from Shrewsbury to Chester carried over 1,000 people and required three locomotives to haul 39 coaches, stopping for toasts to be drunk and speeches to be made. Shrewsbury and Wrexham celebrated with most of the shops shut and church bells ringing all day.

Unfortunately, when the train arrived at Chester all was not well. No reception had been organised for the party and there was 'neither a biscuit to eat nor a glass with which one could hob nob with another'! By the time the train was ready to return to Shrewsbury it must have been quite a spectacle. Another 20 carriages had been added and two more engines were needed to pull it. Following the failure over a reception at Chester it was now running two hours late.

A year later, in 1849, there were bitter quarrels between the London & North Western Railway (LNWR) and the Great Western Railway (GWR) over access to the lines around Chester. With the LNWR controlling approach lines from Euston to Wolverhampton, the company expected the Shrewsbury &

131

All that remains of Rossett station today is a crumbling platform edge. The station closed on 29th October 1964 with freight closure four years later. (Author)

Birmingham Railway (S&BR) and its neighbour the S&CR to fall into its hands. To combat the threat, the S&BR and the S&CR made a traffic agreement with Birkenhead, Lancashire & Cheshire Junction Railway (BL&CJR), to challenge the LNWR and also develop traffic between Merseyside, the Black Country and South Wales. The LNWR issued an ultimatum to the S&BR and the S&CR which they rejected. Unfortunately for the S&CR the LNWR had a majority on the Chester station joint committee who instructed ticket offices to refuse bookings for passengers wishing to travel to Wolverhampton via Shrewsbury. During disturbances that followed, the S&CR's booking clerk was thrown out of his office.

In his book, *A Regional History of the Railways of Great Britain, North and Mid Wales,* Peter E. Baughan described what happened next. Under pressure, the BL&CJR gave way to the LNWR approach and discouraged S&CR passengers on its own lines by arranging connections at impossible hours. In reply the S&CR

132

Balderton station seen here after closure to passengers in March 1952. From 1896 until the 1940s Balderton was linked to Eaton Hall by a private narrow-gauge railway. (Lens of Sutton)

ran omnibuses to Chester from Birkenhead, only to find them barred from Chester station yard by 'gangs of LNWR toughs' who also defaced S&CR timetables and posters. It took many more months of such activities before the BL&CJR shareholders complained and the S&CR was once again allowed access over BL&CJR rails to Birkenhead.

Meantime the GWR was pressing northwards seeking access to Merseyside. In desperation the S&BR and the S&CR turned to the GWR at Paddington for support, forming a traffic agreement in January 1851. Further skirmishes with the LNWR followed but the S&CR refused to bow to pressure.

In 1852 Parliament agreed a Bill whereby a joint S&BR and S&CR managing committee was extended to include the GWR. During 1853 struggles continued. In 1854 Parliament agreed an Amalgamation Act whereby the GWR effectively gained control of the two smaller companies and the LNWR conceded defeat. GWR lines had reached Chester. Attempts by the GWR to build broad gauge (7' 0") tracks failed with the line from Birmingham

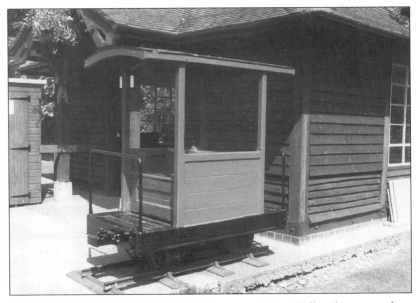

An original brake van from the narrow-gauge Eaton Hall railway seen here during a centenary exhibition held at Chester's Grosvenor Park during 1996. It was built at Duffield Works near Derby in 1895. (Author)

via Shrewsbury becoming the first GWR 'narrow gauge' (subsequently considered standard gauge) to be constructed.

Travelling southwards from Chester and after leaving the main line to Holyhead the first station was Saltney, a basic wooden structure which survived only until 1960. Next came Balderton which linked with a private narrow-gauge railway connecting with Eaton Hall. The 15 inch gauge line was built in 1896 at the instigation of the Duke of Westminster so that coal and supplies could be conveyed to Eaton Hall. Locomotives and rolling stock were constructed by Sir Arthur Heywood at Duffield Bank, near Derby, and the track was laid on cast iron sleepers to Heywood's design. The line was just under three miles in length plus a branch to the estate works at Cuckoo's Nest.

Nothing remains of the line today between Balderton and Eaton Hall where the grounds are strictly private. When scrapped in the 1940s the track went to the Romney, Hythe &

Name plates from the narrow-gauge locomotives used on the former Eaton Hall Railway displayed at the Chester Grosvenor Park exhibition. 'Katie' was named after a former Duchess of Westminster. (Author)

Dymchurch Railway in Kent and to the Ravenglass & Eskdale Railway in Cumbria. An original brake van, built at Duffield Works near Derby in 1895, has survived and this could be seen at a centenary exhibition held at Chester's Grosvenor Park from May to August 1996.

Next on the S&CR came Pulford station. It only lasted a few years, closing in 1855 for passengers, but continued for goods as Pulford siding until 1959. Although the area has no great railway history, Pulford gained notoriety during the Civil War when Chester was besieged by the Roundheads. It was reported that the people of Pulford smuggled food to the starving city, sometimes through Dodleston and sometimes via Eaton and the river.

Rossett lasted longer – until October 1964. Of the station only one platform edge has survived. Gresford came next, once part of a thriving coal mining area. Many will recall the terrible pit

Saltney station, a basic wooden construction, on the line from Chester to Ruabon and Shrewsbury. The station closed in 1960. (Lens of Sutton)

disaster in September 1934 when many lives were lost.

Further south came Wrexham General, Wrexham being a town which at one time enjoyed three railway stations (see chapter 11). Onwards towards Shrewsbury the principal stations were (and still are) Ruabon, Chirk and Gobowen. It was from Chirk that Glyn Valley Tramway (GVT) freight services began in 1873 along the Ceiriog valley, on 2 ft 4 in narrow-gauge track just constructed from Chirk's Gledrid Wharf on the Shropshire Union Canal to Glyn Ceiriog in what was once Denbighshire. Coaches and wagons were initially horse drawn.

During the 60 years or so of the tramway's existence, the company did little to encourage the passenger traffic which began a year later in 1874. It took just under one hour to cover the six mile journey and a comic postcard of the day claimed the tramway's motto was 'No hurry or worry' and that 'ten minute stops were made to pick flowers!'

The tramway survived until 1933 for passengers and 1935 for freight with closure forced by competition from road traffic. When passenger traffic ceased in 1933 the tramway was carrying an average of only seven people daily. There are numerous

Ruabon station in the 1960s when passengers could catch trains to Llangollen, Bala, Barmouth as well as Chester or Shrewsbury. (Lens of Sutton)

reminders of the GVT but perhaps the best can be found at the Talyllyn Railway at Towyn. Two former Glyn Valley coaches operate as first class accommodation, superbly restored to their former GVT livery.

The station at Gobowen is unique. When in December 1992 British Rail withdrew the booking office facility, three students at Moreton Hall School for Girls decided it should not close. On July 5th 1993, in a blaze of national publicity, Moreton Hall Travel took over. Initially girls from Moreton Hall School served as directors, sold tickets and announced trains. They even repainted the booking office and waiting room. Today the station is independently run by a company known as Severn-Dee Travel (named after the two rivers).

Some 145 years later, the line from Chester to Shrewsbury still exists although in a much diminished form. Part of it has been singled and many stations have gone, with those remaining inadequately used. But before leaving Shrewsbury, the signal box is more than worth a mention. Built by the LNWR in 1903 and dominating the north-western end of Shrewsbury station, it is 96 ft 6 ins long and houses 180 levers. The box controls a busy triangular junction and is helped by four adjacent boxes. It is the largest box, both structurally and in lever frame size, on today's Railtrack.

The late Robert Adley MP, a past rail enthusiast, once suggested to the then Prime Minister, Margaret Thatcher, that she should visit the Shrewsbury box when next in the town. It was an offer she sadly declined.

14
Southwards Into Shropshire

Crewe/Nantwich/Shrewsbury
Nantwich/Audlem/Market Drayton/Wellington
Tattenhall junction/Malpas/Whitchurch

Crewe/Nantwich/Shrewsbury

The 32½ mile Shrewsbury & Crewe Railway, built by the London & North Western Railway (LNWR), was approved by Parliament on 20th August 1853. It was part of the LNWR's endeavours to reach Mid Wales whilst also supporting Welsh

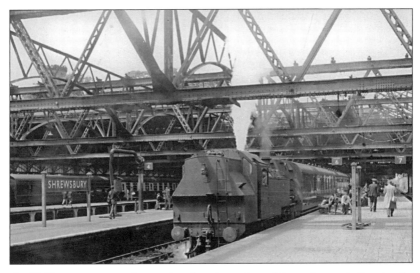

A GWR passenger train awaits departure from Shrewsbury station in the early 1960s. The wide span roof was a prominent feature of Shrewsbury station but this was removed in 1963 due to its deteriorating condition. (D.K. Jones Collection)

139

Nantwich in the 1960s, a station still surviving between Crewe and Whitchurch. This became a junction in 1863 when a GWR branch reached the town from Market Drayton. (Lens of Sutton)

promoters to reach the Cambrian coast. Engineers for the project were Joseph Locke and J.E. Errington with construction delayed over several years due to disputes about the approach to Shrewsbury. When the line opened on 1st September 1858, it proved a boon to Nantwich residents. Previously their only access to a railway had been a station some two miles to the north on the Chester & Crewe Railway (C&CR) but the Shrewsbury line carried rails right into the town centre. The C&CR station was renamed Worleston (chapter 3).

The line was single track but doubling soon followed to cater for increasing traffic. Travelling from Crewe there was a small halt at Gresty (serving Gresty Green) but this closed soon after World War I. Willaston came next but today trains race through to Nantwich since Willaston closed to passengers in December 1954. Nantwich became a busy junction when in October 1863 a Great Western Railway (GWR) line (built by the Nantwich & Market Drayton Railway) reached the town from Market Drayton. Four years later, in October 1867, GWR trains could

Wrenbury station close to the Cheshire/Shropshire border. Today it is a request stop only, serving trains between Crewe and Shrewsbury with many going on to Cardiff Central. (Lens of Sutton)

reach Wellington, giving connections with Shrewsbury and Birmingham.

After Wrenbury (a station still surviving) trains reach Whitchurch in North Shropshire. This increased in importance when the Cambrian Railways opened a line on 27th July 1864 giving connections into Wales. Whitchurch survives but the Cambrian lines have gone. Today at Whitchurch the trackwork has been simplified and the station modernised. Only a few sidings remain yet railcars still pass through, providing a service between Crewe and Shrewsbury with a number travelling on to Cardiff. Between Whitchurch and Shrewsbury, stations still exist at Prees, Wem and Yorton whereas Hadnall station closed in 1960.

In the early 1950s the Shrewsbury and Crewe line was worked by fine steam locomotives such as the class 8P Pacific no 46202 *Princess Anne*. In his book, *Rail Centres: Crewe*, Rex Christiansen reminds us that the *Princess Anne* was destroyed on 8th October 1952 in the terrible rail disaster at Harrow & Wealdstone when as many as 112 lives were lost plus ten who died later from their

Formerly an LNWR station, Prees in Shropshire on the Crewe to Shrewsbury line is still open. This picture was taken after 'grouping' in the early 1920s. (Lens of Sutton)

Whitchurch, at one time a busy junction with direct services to Chester, Crewe and Shrewsbury. Whitchurch was also the terminus for Cambrian Railways services to Ellesmere, Oswestry and beyond. (Lens of Sutton)

142

Today Whitchurch's branch lines have gone, the station has been modernised and the trackwork simplified. A former signal box beyond the station survives. (Author)

injuries. As a result of this accident, express trains were temporarily diverted to Paddington via Nantwich and Wellington over former GWR lines.

Nantwich/Audlem/ Market Drayton/Wellington

On 7th June 1861 Parliament approved the Nantwich & Market Drayton Railway. A year later on 7th August 1862 the Wellington & Drayton Railway was incorporated. Both companies were GWR supported, which considered the connections to be of considerable importance giving access to both Crewe and

Stoke-on-Trent. There had previously been a number of unsuccessful schemes in the area including the Sheffield, Shrewsbury & South Wales Direct Railway which planned a route via Leek, Whitmore (crossing the main Crewe/Stafford line), Market Drayton and Hodnet. The GWR was anxious to thwart plans submitted, also it opposed a proposal submitted by the Wellington & Cheshire Junction Railway for a line from Wellington to Market Drayton, Nantwich and Northwich.

The 11 mile long branch from Nantwich to Market Drayton came first, opening on 20th October 1863, and four years later, on 16th October 1867, the Market Drayton to Wellington section of just over 16 miles was completed. The through route was classed as a secondary main line, stations were far apart and passengers were few. Three years later the North Staffordshire Railway (NSR) reached Market Drayton from Stoke, a line which served the industrial areas west of Stoke-on-Trent.

Market Drayton derived the first part of its name from the markets that have been held there for over 750 years. Each

The first trains to reach Market Drayton came from Nantwich in 1863. When a line from Market Drayton opened to Wellington four years later, GWR trains could reach Crewe. (Lens of Sutton)

144

Audlem on the Market Drayton to Nantwich branch, an area better known today for its canal and locks. When rail traffic dwindled in the early 1930s, the GWR opened halts to encourage passengers but this did not prove successful. (Lens of Sutton)

Wednesday it is possible to join in a bustling, bargain hunting tradition in traffic-free streets and under the old Buttercross. One of the town's celebrated products is gingerbread, faithful to recipes up to 200 years old and made by the local bakers' shops.

In the early 1920s there were six stopping trains each way on weekdays between Wellington and Nantwich and only one on Sundays. In an effort to increase passenger traffic in the early 1930s, the GWR opened seven halts but it did little to help. The line became considerably busier during electrification of the main line from London through Crewe and for a time its prospects loked good. But this did not last and the familiar downward trend followed. Passenger services survived until 9th September 1963.

There were two intermediate stations between Nantwich and Market Drayton, these being Audlem and Adderley. It was near Audlem that the railway criss-crossed the Shropshire-Cheshire

145

Malpas between Whitchurch and Chester on a short 15 mile branch between Whitchurch and Waverton (on the Crewe/Chester line). The branch was popular for a time with commuters to Chester or even Liverpool. (Lens of Sutton)

border. The area is perhaps better known today for its canal and series of locks. Audlem station was completely obliterated after closure of the line and it is difficult today to determine exactly where it existed. Even the nearby road bridge has gone.

A final indignity came to the branch when it was suggested that the Market Drayton to Nantwich stretch might become a walkway. Whereas the short section from Wellington became part of the Silkin Way, local authorities in Cheshire were less co-operative, considering the trackbed to be unsuitable.

Tattenhall junction/Malpas/ Whitchurch

The short 15 mile branch from Tattenhall junction (on the line

Tattenhall station on the former Whitchurch/Waverton branch which closed in 1957 to become a private residence. Tattenhall had two stations, Tattenhall Road on the main Crewe line closed later in 1966. (Author)

from Chester to Crewe) to Whitchurch was opened by the LNWR on 1st October 1872 but it was never extensively used. It was planned as a route to compete against the GWR monopoly between Shrewsbury and Chester but it had little impact. There were three stations, Tattenhall, Broxton and Malpas and a halt at Grindley Brook. The line through peaceful countryside with little potential closed to passengers on 16th September 1957.

The first station southwards was Tattenhall which at one time had two stations, the other on the Chester/Crewe line. With train services giving easy access to Chester or even Liverpool, the area became popular with many businessmen who could easily commute by train. It is said that a stationmaster from the 19th century would never let a train depart if he heard a commuter's pony and trap hurrying along the road. Tattenhall on the

147

Malpas station closed to passengers in September 1957 and to goods in November 1963. Today the building retains its former dignity thanks to Miles Macadam, a road surfacing company, which has faithfully kept the station's identity. (Author)

Whitchurch/Chester line closed in 1957 so Tattenhall Road on the main line was renamed just Tattenhall until it too closed in 1966.

Next came Broxton. The station has gone and the area has become a lorry and car park as well as a picnic site. All that remains from the past is a crane base behind the lorry park. Broxton was once a busy station with trains transporting cattle, sheep, horses and vegetables. Seasonal fruit came from market gardens at Farndon and Holt to leave Broxton, arriving at Manchester's Smithfield Market for sale the same day. Close to the nearby Egerton Arms stand a number of trees. These were planted by Bamber & Sons, cheese manufacturers, to shelter the trackside cheese warehouses in hot weather.

Malpas station building looks today much as it did before its closure except that it has become the offices for Miles Macadam, a road surfacing company. The track may have gone but signs

148

still say 'Trains to Chester' and doors are marked 'Station Master's Office' or 'Ticket Office'. One leaves Malpas station wondering why so many closed stations remain at such a high standard compared with neglected live stations!

15

A Line From Chester To Denbigh

Chester/Saltney Ferry/Broughton/Mold
Mold to Denbigh

Passenger services from Chester to Mold commenced in August 1849 with traffic also including considerable quantities of freight. Mold station seen here in LNWR days c1910 before motor cars took over. (Lens of Sutton)

Chester/Saltney Ferry/Broughton/Mold

During the early days of the Mold Railway, passengers were hardly encouraged by a note in a timetable which read, 'Company arrangements incomplete – accuracy doubtful'!

Mold residents had pressed hard for a rail outlet, first petitioning the directors of the Chester & Holyhead Railway to

150

The remains of Padeswood & Buckley station on the former Chester to Mold line after its closure in 1958. (Lens of Sutton)

bring a line through the valley. Earlier the Shrewsbury & Chester Railway had lodged a Bill for a branch but this was defeated. The Mold Railway Company was formed in 1847 although completion of the line was threatened more than once through lack of funds. It was the prospect of lucrative mineral traffic that finally got the town its railway.

The Mold Railway from Chester (Saltney junction) commenced services on 14th August 1849 with intermediate stations at Broughton, Hope and Llong. The line was worked by the London & North Western Railway (LNWR) and in the early days trains were mixed passenger and freight. Later in 1849 the branch had the luxury of its own locomotive. Named *Mammoth*, it was a 2-4-0 tank engine built at Crewe and numbered 247.

Mineral traffic, estimated at up to 800,000 tons annually, began in earnest when a branch opened to Ffrith. Initially tracks had reached only as far as Coed Talon where a private railway connected with Nerquis Colliery. The branch to Ffrith opened in November 1849 worked by quarry owner, Edward Oakley, with his locomotive *Diamond*. Mold Railway traffic benefited when new coal pits opened at Coed Talon in 1861 and

151

The line from Mold to Denbigh took eight years to build but hopes to provide a direct alternative route to Rhyl did not materialise. In the early 1920s over a dozen trains each way daily passed through Nannerch station, seen here. (Lens of Sutton)

Leeswood Colliery in 1863. Around the same period industrial development in Mold increased the town's population to over 12,000.

Trains between Chester and Mold had to cope with many severe gradients and the 1 in 43 incline between Broughton and Hope caused many accidents. These were mostly due to the stalling of under-powered locomotives. On the mineral line between Coppa and Ffrith the gradient was put to good use allowing loaded wagons to free-wheel down to storage sidings.

Regular passenger services came to an end on 30th April 1962.

Mold to Denbigh

The railway from Mold to Denbigh, agreed by Parliament on August 6th 1861, was a line that nearly did not happen. With a line already in existence from Chester along the Dee Estuary to Rhyl and beyond (opened in 1844), investors questioned the need for this additional route over sparsely populated areas.

152

Denbigh station which once served trains to Chester, Corwen or Rhyl. Like Mold, the former station site gave way mainly to a supermarket and part of the trackbed was used to improve the Rhyl/Pentrefoelas main road. (Lens of Sutton)

Nevertheless the Directors of the Mold & Denbigh Junction Railway (M&DJR) pressed ahead with plans for a 17 mile line through the narrow valleys of the Alyn and Wheeler. There was even a proposal for a spur which would provide direct access to Rhyl via the Vale of Clwyd Railway. Although partially built it was never completed.

Like the Mold Railway, it ran into difficulties during construction caused by a 1866 financial crisis. Work stopped and there were appeals to landowners not to press for compensation. In June 1869 Mold residents witnessed riots around a railway bridge on the nearly-completed line to Denbigh. Rioters seized the bridge as a vantage point to attack soldiers who were endeavouring to remove, by train, colliers in dispute with the Leeswood Coal Company.

The line from Mold to Denbigh opened for regular passenger traffic on 12th September 1869. Surprisingly, the railway was

153

Mold station before its closure to passengers in April 1962. The buildings have long since been demolished, the site currently occupied by Tesco's supermarket. (Lens of Sutton)

mainly double track whereas the routes it joined were single track only. Time did prove however that double track was justified, for the passenger service was to reach double the average branch line intensity.

There were intermediate stations at Rhydymwyn, Nannerch, Caerwys and Bodfari. Certain trains also stopped at Star Crossing Halt (534 ft above sea level) between Rhydymwyn and Nannerch. At Nannerch a wall had to be built to separate the railway from the road to avoid passing vehicle-horses becoming frightened! The idea of a spur bypassing Denbigh to provide direct services to Rhyl was not forgotten. Applications for powers to complete the link were resubmitted in 1906 and 1914 but the proposal was never carried out.

Despite LNWR backing, the M&DJR remained independent throughout. At that time about a dozen trains each weekday served passengers between Chester, Mold, Denbigh and on to Corwen, although few would have taken the complete route, preferring the faster GWR service from Chester to Corwen via Wrexham.

154

The entire line from Chester to Denbigh closed to passengers in April 1962. The LNWR Bodfari station, photographed c1910, was the last intermediate station before Denbigh. (Lens of Sutton)

As road traffic increased, so the number of passengers fell. By the early 1960s the line, like so many others, was considered redundant and was closed. As with the Chester/Mold line, passenger traffic from Mold to Denbigh came to an end on 30th April 1962.

After closure Denbigh station area gave way mainly to a supermarket and part of the trackbed was used to improve the Rhyl-Pentrefoelas main road. Many intermediate stations became private residences although Nannerch station building was demolished to straighten a stretch of the A541. Mold station close to the river Alyn has completely gone. If you should be shopping in the town's Tesco supermarket today, you could be standing close to where townsfolk once stood waiting for a train to Denbigh or Chester.

In other instances overbridges have been removed where the motor car has taken priority. It seems surprising that, so comparatively recently after closure, many young folk today hardly realise that such a railway ever existed.

Conclusion

When 'grouping' came under the 1921 Railway Act, the four main railways formed were the London, Midland & Scottish (LMS), London & North Eastern (LNER), Great Western (GWR) and the Southern (SR). In Cheshire, the London & North Western Railway and the Midland Railway became part of the LMS. GWR lines retained their own identity. The Great Central Railway and the Great Northern Railway became part of the LNER. We have already read that since the Cheshire Lines Committee comprised members from both the newly formed LMS and the LNER, it was allowed to retain its independence.

Throughout the 1920s and 1930s many branches went into decline. Buses were able to offer a more flexible service than the trains and road haulage was on the increase. In addition the private motor car was beginning to make its presence felt. Nationalisation followed in 1948. The railways, still recovering from the demands of war service, were slow to meet any competition and were losing ground. Reduced revenue led to increased economies and then closures, with the entire pattern of inland transport gradually changing.

In March 1963 proposals were made in a report which became popularly known as the 'Beeching Plan'. Basically the idea was to keep lines considered essential and give up the remainder. It was claimed that one third of the rail system in Britain carried only 1% of the total traffic. Drastic cuts followed and many more lines disappeared. Closures – at first a trickle – became a torrent. Where branches once existed, some linking major routes across the region, soon only the original trunk routes remained. A few branch lines have survived but their future must surely be considered uncertain.

When rail privatisation came in the mid-1990s, rail travellers were told it would give them an exciting future. Yet press reports continually indicate that 'complaints about late, cancelled and overcrowded trains have soared [and] figures point to an alarming deterioration in services'. And this view is endorsed by the need for continuing track repairs and with ever increasing rail fares. The Channel Tunnel, although providing rapid links with European capitals, still has to prove itself financially.

At the present time continuing financial losses on the railways appear inevitable. Perhaps there is comfort in the fact that further widespread closures on the scale previously suffered would be politically unacceptable today. Presumably heavy government subsidies will continue and, will no doubt, increase in the years to come.

From the days of Cheshire's early turnpikes and tollgates, time has taken us through the canal age to the railway age. 'Railway mania' is now well behind us and we are back to the roads once again with cars and motorways a part of present day life. Yet already many roads and motorways are quite inadequate for the task intended, with lorries continually increasing in weight and the volume of traffic reaching ever higher proportions. Surely those who closed down so many of our branch lines have much to answer for.

It is difficult at the present time to foresee the railway's future. One of the main disadvantages is that its future is in the hands of politicians. Sadly the days have gone when the railways provided an efficient unified service and when railway employees could take a real pride in their work.

Surely the late Sir Edward Watkin, pioneer of so many railway schemes including the Cheshire Lines Committee, would turn in his grave at the thought of many of today's happenings!

INDEX